The Butterfly Chronicles

A JOURNEY OF RADICAL TRANSFORMATION

L. NICOLE CERVANTES, M.S.W.

Knowledge Power Books
www.knowledgepowerbooks.com

ISBN: 978-09981701-3-8
Library of Congress Control Number: 2017934777

Edited by: Laurel J. Davis
Cover Design: Juan Roberts, Creative Lunacy, Inc.
Literary Director: Sandra L. Slayton

Published by:
Knowledge Power Books
A Division of Knowledge Power Communications, Inc.
Valencia, California 91355
www.knowledgepowerbooks.com

Printed in the United States of America

Dedication

LEARNING HOW TO GROW IN GRACE

This book is dedicated to the five angels God gave me the grace to mother: Poket, Sweet Pea, Baby Girl, Destiny and Purpose.

Contents

My Tears Are Not in Vain

Close your eyes
Unwind your mind
Allow our souls to connect
Through these pages
The mysteries of life
And all the secrets we try to forget
I stand not afraid in my truth
Not a villain of pain
Not a victim of shame
I am confident
I know without a doubt
My tears are not in vain.

CHAPTER 1

Reflections

"Whew," Seanette exclaimed, letting out a gasp of both relief and pain. She searched her mind for a solution. She was afraid but also determined to finally move forward—to protect and defend herself by any means necessary. This time, it would be different. She then remembered the butcher knife she stored for protection underneath her mattress. Frantically, she lifted the mattress and was immediately reassured to discover the knife was still there. Looking at her reflection on the blade, she wondered, "How did it come to this?" Throughout her entire life, she had these kinds of conversations with herself. Sometimes she didn't know the answers. And other times she did, answers not only to the problems but how she got there. Still, she ran, and she ran, and she ran, trying to lose herself. Ha! She lost herself, alright. She just never imagined that the thing she was trying to lose was the thing she should have cherished the most: HERSELF!

Seanette closed her eyes, leaving behind Los Angeles' San Fernando Valley and the year 2001, along with all the previous years of trauma, mistakes and heartaches. Instead, she went back to 1982 and Leimert Park, a community in Los Angeles which was always a pleasant reference point, a place and time of comfort. That year marked a period in her life that she still considered to be "happy times." It was a time when she could be free, without judgment or ridicule, just her and her Big Wheel. She rode that thing along Leimert Park's pristine sidewalks with nothing on her mind but just enjoying the sun and the breeze as it gently blew her hair. In her world, she felt sheltered from the trouble around her. Nothing else mattered when she was cruising on her Big Wheel. She played hide-and-seek with the wind and hid from the trees and plants. Even though their shadows always told her hiding places, she still had fun.

The flowers were Seanette's allies. They seemed to communicate with her by gently brushing up against her skin, as if to confirm her safety. Seanette adored the different flowers and roses in her neighborhood. She would stare at the rose petals for hours and wonder how, even after the rain, God got the color and scent to stay on. Her best friends were ladybugs and butterflies. She was fascinated by these beautiful, harmless insects and often held conversations with them, pretending they would tell her about their world. But out of these two creatures made by God, she admired the butterfly the most.

Seanette loved watching every stage the caterpillar went through to become the beautiful butterfly. She allowed the caterpillar to tickle her as it crawled on her hands and wrists, and she would squirm like a worm and hold her stomach trying not to laugh. She would watch in eager anticipation how the caterpillar prepared its cocoon. It never crossed her mind that it was a vital and necessary process for this miraculous transformation; she assumed it was more like a resting place. And in some regards, it was.

As fascinating as the process was, though, Seanette was more interested in knowing what was going on inside the cocoon. She didn't have the patience to wait until the process was complete. She thought it was time-consuming and tiresome. Oh, how she wished she were a butterfly, able to fly away from everything and leave nothing behind but a shell. She was always both frustrated and excited whenever she saw a butterfly aloft in the wind. It was thrilling to gently capture and support the butterfly in her hands for a few minutes. She even dedicated a made-up lullaby to the butterfly species and, after singing the song, she would release the ravishing creature and watch it flutter away.

Seanette's imaginary world was suddenly disrupted. "Sean . . . ! Seanette!" Pam's familiar voice reverberated through Seanette's spirit, causing the flowers, the ladybugs, the butterflies, the wind, and even the tattle-telling plants to retreat back into the real world. Pam had a way of calling Seanette's name that made everything come to an immediate halt. It was in those disruptive moments that Seanette always felt she had to become another person, a person no longer care-free but who had to be on guard. So, she put on a coat of sorts, one she kept on for years, refusing to take it off. But eventually she removed it and discarded it, with pleasure. What coat? The coat of fear, suicidal thoughts, pride, rebellion, hate, judgment, shame, guilt, low self-esteem, sexual abuse, physical abuse, domestic violence, anger and pain. Nevertheless, whenever Pam called for her, Seanette had to answer. She never knew what Pam wanted, but she knew she had to respond. When Pam called, Seanette's entire body became tense and hot like fire. Seanette became so accustomed to being nervous that she thought it was just a part of her personality.

If it wasn't clear by now, Pam was Seanette's mother. Pamela Ethel Brandon was her birth name, but to her friends, she was just plain Pam. To have an opinion was not tolerated. All of Seanette's thoughts were subject to judgment, and usually, Pam didn't agree. She never agreed. Seanette never knew what kind of mood her mother would be in, because she could turn her feelings on and off like a light switch. The signs usually changed pretty frequently, but there were always two main things Seanette looked for. One was the company her mother entertained, and the other was music.

For as long as Seanette could remember, music was always playing in the house. Although the volume was usually several decibels higher than it needed to be, music was welcomed and loved in the home like a family member. It served as therapy for Pam, a way for her to escape from everything around her, because her feelings always dictated what would be played. Music was her first love, and drugs were her second. If Stevie Wonder, Maze featuring Frankie Beverly, Earth, Wind & Fire, Chaka Khan, Eddie Kendricks, Donny Hathaway, The Commodores or Leroy Hutson was playing, it was a sign that she was a little tipsy but feeling good. If Rick James, Bootsy Collins, War, Millie Jackson, Betty Wright, Tina Turner, Michael Henderson, Aretha Franklin, Al Green, Sade or Marvin Gaye was playing, that was a sign that she was depressed and generally had taken too many drugs or drunk too much alcohol.

Either way, Pam didn't need an artist to influence her to get loaded—the music just enhanced the mood. She had a serious love affair with drugs. Marijuana was her first drug of choice, and throughout the years other drugs just seemed to attach themselves to her pain—from PCP to snorting cocaine, to mixing marijuana with cocaine (which was called a "primo"), to freebasing and, lastly, to alcohol.

Seanette knew upon entering the house what illicit substance her mother had indulged in that day. She knew the smell of every drug and the side effects they had on her mother. She could also pretty much tell by her mother's body language what kind of day or night she was going to have. If Pam had just smoked a joint and had a glass of wine, she was mellow—nothing to fear. If she had been drinking liquor, Seanette had better watch out! Pam would yell at her and a whoopin' wouldn't be far behind. Or, Pam would display awkward, even morbid forms of love by suddenly offering hugs and kisses in the midst of her uncontrollable crying.

If Pam smoked PCP, she was like a zombie, unable to comprehend or function. This meant that Seanette was safe from harm, but also that her mother's mental state was a constant worry. If Pam snorted a few lines or, for that matter, used cocaine in any form, Seanette had to stay alert because her mother would get highly obnoxious and careless and behaved erratically. Some examples of her behavior included cussing Seanette out, giving her a whoopin', or rattling off a list of unreasonable chores for Seanette to complete ASAP, which often left Seanette confused!

The worst time of all was when Pam was sober. She was always easily frustrated and irritated when she was sober. As much as Seanette wished and prayed for her mother to stop using drugs, the reality was that's when it was much harder to deal with her. She was not accustomed to Pam just being herself, it was just too unpredictable because anything could set her off. It could be the bus being late picking her up, Seanette not bringing her a glass of cold water or food fast enough, or even Seanette needing help with her homework. In any case, Pam's reaction could be anything, which made Seanette feel constantly on the lookout.

Seanette developed a system of defining the severity of Pam's drug usage on the basis of her mother's past patterns of actions and reactions. If Pam was just smoking weed, Seanette didn't see that as a serious drug. Both of her parents taught her that "Weed is not a drug; it grows from the earth, so it's an herb used to calm and relax nerves." Seanette hated the smell of marijuana, and she just didn't understand how both of her parents would just smoke it in front of her like it was an acceptable routine. In fact, it became a part of their everyday ritual.

One time when Seanette was in second grade, a few police officers from the D.A.R.E. program came to her school. The first thing they showed was a marijuana joint, claiming it was a drug. Later that same day, Pam and Seanette were cruising down Edgehill Street in their 1978, avocado green, convertible Cadillac Eldorado, when Pam opened the ashtray, pulled out half of a joint and lit it up. Seanette jumped at the chance to share with her what transpired earlier that day at school. "Momma," she said, the police came to our school today, and they said that marijuana was a drug." Pam quickly pulled over to the side of the road, almost choking from the smoke as she took a toke, and replied, "This is not a drug. I don't care what the police say. You hear? Marijuana is an herb, and it grows from the earth. Now don't ever let me hear you say that again." Seanette trusted and loved her mother dearly, but at the same time, she was skeptical because she looked at the police as real-life super heroes.

Seanette made several careful mental notes that day: Never ask her mother questions or share what she heard. Always remain silent, no matter what happens to, around or directly in front of her. And finally, it was all a figment of her imagination to think anything else. From that day forward, Seanette never voiced her opinion or concerns about drugs to her mother because, apparently, it was a form of disrespect or betrayal to Pam. Besides, since Pam took the time to explain to Seanette the facts about marijuana, Seanette didn't think it was bad.

However, the other drugs made Seanette feel like she was in constant competition for her mother's attention. The PCP was one of many that Seanette hated. When Pam used PCP, she seemed lifeless. Her body stood erect and stiff, her eyes dilated, and when she did try to function, she would move literally in slow motion. It was also difficult for her to communicate. Seanette would desperately try to talk to her, "Momma, are you all right?" saying three or four times, "Momma, Momma, Momma." Pam would turn her neck slowly towards Seanette while trying to wiggle her fingers or move her other limbs, a sign to Seanette that her mother was desperately trying to be coherent. She would repeatedly clear her throat and part her lips as if to respond, only to say one word to console Seanette's heart: "Yeah." Then she'd be snatched back into another world, a foreign land where her soul alone could abide. Seanette concluded that at some level her mother wanted to be dead, she wanted to escape totally from this world and all her ghastly pain. Seanette's youthful, naïve mind could not even imagine or comprehend what great pain Pam had suffered in her life.

Seanette often wondered, what circumstances could have been so bad that she couldn't help fix her momma? How could she help her get back all that she lost: her youth, her innocence and her self-esteem? What were her momma's dreams and hopes? Who stole them from her and, more importantly, why?

In any case, during her early adolescent years, Seanette yearned for the times her mother did smile. She longed for her momma's touch. She longed for her momma's laugh. She missed those occasional times when her momma would let her sit on the back of the couch to comb and play with her hair, and the special trips to the library where Pam would pick out books for her that challenged her literacy skills or nurtured her adventurous imagination or encouraged her to be a dreamer.

Seanette wished she and her mother could once again share their laughs and tears together, like when they were reciting the lines from one of their favorite movies, such as "Sparkle," "Terms of Endearment," "The Wiz" or "Imitation of Life." Sadly, all she could do was reminisce. As Seanette would study Pam, she imagined her momma cooking her favorite meal—meatloaf, brussel sprouts and mashed potatoes, topped off with a bubbling hot peach crisp for dessert.

Oh, how Seanette's heart overflowed with joy when she would sing songs with her mother like a backup singer. Pam would get two hairbrushes and, like a duo sisters' group, they would perform in front of their make-believe crowd. "Hey, Rock Bottom"—that's what her momma called her—"you got to move your hips back and forth like the waves of the ocean." And then she would ask Seanette to be a "special helper" by letting her rinse the dishes after she washed them.

Seanette savored her natural high during these special moments, and it didn't matter if she had to share it with a twelve-ounce can of malt liquor or a glass of wine and a marijuana joint. It was far better than that soul-seizing snare of a fowler drug, PCP. When Pam was high on PCP, Seanette wanted so much to know how to help her, if only she could reach her. But she couldn't. And this often left her sad, frustrated and angry because she loved her momma so much. Just one look at her and Seanette knew, and she hated it. That . . . that drug that drifted her momma away from her. Why?

Many times, Seanette would just look at her mother and watch, wishing she could have her for just that moment. She wanted just to hold her and tell her it was going to be okay. She just wanted her momma to talk about whatever the pain was so she could understand. For years, though, it was only in Seanette's head that she played out this dialogue with her mother, over and over again.

Initially, PCP was the only drug Seanette did not blame her mother for using. Instead, she blamed the unseen, untouched and unknown pain. As Pam's addictive behavior grew worse and her cravings for a variety of different drugs surfaced, Seanette began to hate and judge her, and eventually lost compassion and love for her. Seanette also became an extreme introvert. It would be a long road of her own experiences and similar abuse before she would understand her mother's pain.

Finding Pam's paraphernalia around the house was nothing new. She often left razor blades, saucers and cut-up pieces of drinking straws, which were her tools for snorting cocaine. Once while playing detective, Seanette found her mother's little velvet case containing a miniature gold spoon used for "tooting." And the little brown glass bottles in her nightstand drawers contained cocaine residue or the liquid form of PCP, commonly known by the street term "water." She also had boxes of brown Nat Sherman cigarettes, which would be dipped in the PCP. And there were lighters with the tops broken off, used as a "torch" for lighting a cocaine pipe.

Seanette was often with her mother on drug transactions. She was usually left in the car while Pam met with her dealer. Initially, Pam would take just a few minutes, and like a puppy waiting for its master to return, Seanette would wait eagerly for her. But then a few minutes would turn into hours. Sometimes Seanette would watch the sunset, and sometimes, dawn would turn into dusk. She often fell asleep, awakened only by the chill of the night or hunger pangs.

During those times, she hoped her mother would somehow feel her frustrations and remember her in the car, but it never happened. Just sitting there predicting how the evening would go, Seanette wanted to go inside the person's house and just ask if she could take her mother home, but the fear of getting hit or badgered was always present. Eventually, Pam would return to the car, intoxicated.

These experiences left Seanette with a multitude of worries and burdens that should have been a parent's to handle, such as making dinner or even figuring out what they were going to do if there wasn't any food. Getting homework done was always stressful for Seanette, especially math homework. God forbid if she needed help. It didn't matter if her mother was high or not, the outcome was always the same. Pam assumed that Seanette should "automatically" know how to do it without help. She would often scream and yell and maybe whoop Seanette if she couldn't do "simple" addition or subtraction problems. As a result, Seanette acquired a great fear of math for many, many years.

On some occasions, Seanette had to assume the role of nurse and take care of her mother, or the role pastor and pray and recite scriptures to get her through a particularly bad episode. Each time, Seanette thought her momma would give up all the drugs and "get it together." But then, once Pam felt better, the whole cycle would start all over again, like nothing ever happened.

Seanette had this indescribable feeling in the pit of her stomach every time she saw her mother under the influence. She was very observant and knew which drugs were used by the different people her mother entertained. That's because, sadly, she became co-dependent at a very young age. She thought it was her fault her mother used drugs and always felt responsible for her, so she made it her business to find out what drug her mother was currently using so that she could predict her behavior. All the while, she often asked Pam—in her own head, of course—"Why do you have to be like this?" It was very hard for her to digest that her mother was an addict.

Despite the fact that Pam used drugs and alcohol for many, many years, she was highly functional. That's why she never took her addiction seriously. Her body seemed to be made out of titanium. She could stay up all night partying with her friends, but you could best believe when daybreak came, she was up in the shower with K-EARTH 101 blaring from the bathroom as she got ready for work. Seanette always felt her mother was invincible.

Pam was smart, witty, efficient and very resourceful. She was a woman who had no problem expressing herself. She had a way with words, and when she talked, the entire room would stop to listen. Pam always knew how to use words to her advantage to make you believe a lie about yourself or to get her needs met—by any means necessary. She could also create for herself an image to fit in with people of any background. It left most of her so-called friends feeling inferior to her, and that was just the way she liked it.

Pam's occupation always changed. She had jobs, not a career. She also always had a hustle or two on the side. She was a jack-of-all-trades who boasted both "street knowledge" and "book knowledge." She had two legal identities, one was her birth name for occupation purposes, and the other, Carmen Nelson, was her street hustle name. She also claimed to have a twin sister.

Seanette often saw her mother and her mother's friends commit several illegal acts, like drug possession, drug dealing and larceny. For instance, they would often apply for credit cards in the neighbors' names and when the card came to the address, they would make cash advances and purchases. They would open an account at the neighbor-hood bank, deposit fraudulent funds into the account, and then make cash withdrawals. They would create payroll checks using a stolen accounting machine and cash them using phony identification. For $50 to $100 a person, Pam would take deceased people's social security numbers from her job to install telephone service at someone's house. She purchased and spent counterfeit food stamps and money. She and her cohorts orchestrated bogus automobile accidents and physical injuries, file false claims with the fake victim's insurance company and receive settlements for which she would get a one-third cut.

Who Am I?

She stands alone like a picked-over item of clothing
at a clearance or garage sale.
Blaming herself, she cries and whispers to her inner being,
"Where did I fail?"
Uncertain she is about the events of her life that will transpire.
Unbeknownst to her innocent soul, she is a clone for hire.
That "somewhere over the rainbow" she wished for will never occur.
All thoughts of love and acceptance she would have to defer.
Today, she can't speak for herself; sentiments will be
Disregarded because she is only a child.
Unfortunately, by her actions she was labeled unruly,
disorderly and wild.
The guilt, shame, rejection and hate,
What did her spirit gain?
Why was this poor little girl allotted so much pain?
Her sweet, bruised soul could not discern
What idiotic examples of love she did learn

CHAPTER 2
Little Lost Girl

P am had a very traumatic childhood. At the age of five, she was separated from her parents, Stanley and Myrtle, after they divorced. She was raised primarily in California with Myrtle's younger sister Diane and Diane's husband Otis. Initially, Pam's maternal side of the family resided in Cleveland, but then Diane, Otis, their son Otis, Jr. and later Diane's six younger siblings relocated to California, as they had heard about all the opportunities the Golden State had to offer. After his discharge from the U.S. Navy, in the mid-1950s Uncle Otis used his GI Bill to purchase a home in the San Fernando Valley.

As a young newlywed couple, Diane and Otis felt the world was their oyster. Otis became a vocational nurse, while Diane worked her way up the career ladder in the aerospace industry. This was a huge accomplishment for someone who didn't have a high school diploma.

The story of how Pam got separated from her parents and why she was never returned to live with her ten siblings in Cleveland, remains a mystery. According to Myrtle, Diane and Otis stole Pam and two of her older brothers, Patrick and Peter, from a New Year's Eve party. Furthermore, Myrtle believed Diane never sent Pam back to Cleveland because Diane was never able to have any more children of her own after she had Otis, Jr., who was eight years older than Pam. All of the family, friends and neighbors knew he had untreated mental health issues, as he showed early signs of schizophrenia that wasn't diagnosed until his teenage years. For this reason, according to Myrtle,

Diane wanted a daughter. After a few years, Otis and Diane sent Patrick and Peter back to Cleveland because they already had a boy, and Pam was left behind.

Now, according to Diane, she and Otis were given consent from both Stanley and Myrtle to temporarily bring the three children with them when they moved to California. Diane insisted she was only trying to help Myrtle, who was supposed to relocate to California after tying up "a few loose ends." But that never happened. Instead, Myrtle made a life with her other children in a housing development located on the east side of Cleveland. Diane never disputed the accusations as to why she didn't return Pam, but she always insisted that Myrtle didn't want her.

Both Myrtle and Diane always stuck to their individual stories. Pam's early recollections were fuzzy because she was so young. However, she revealed to Seanette that upon their arrival to California, Diane and Otis asked her and her brothers if they wanted to call them "Mom" and "Dad." Patrick and Peter settled on calling them "Aunt" and "Uncle." But Pam, being the youngest and most impressionable, with a bit of persuasion (especially after her brothers left) started calling them "Mom" and "Dad." So, when Seanette came along, Diane and Otis were known as "Granny" and "Grandpa."

Diane and Otis were very generous in exposing the children to a life far better than what they had with their mother. Diane enrolled them and Otis, Jr. into a private Catholic school, where they were each adored by the nuns. After a few years, Myrtle went to Child Protective Services (CPS) and accused her sister and brother-in-law of taking her three children to California illegally.

CPS contacted Diane and sent three plane tickets for all three siblings to return to Cleveland. Diane and Otis asked the children if they wanted to stay or return to their birth mother. The boys were old enough to remember their parents, so they wanted to return. Pam has consistently said she doesn't know why, but she wanted to stay. Otis used her ticket to escort the two boys to their mother. When he returned to California, the sexual and physical abuse began.

Violated

Twisted, manipulative actions of being kind
Robbing the innocence
Leaving the residue of guilt and shame
The fear of knowing you intimately
I pray every night to die
No comfort to silence my cries
Feelings sometimes unable to describe
Hidden agendas you show as I close my eyes
Helpless, hopeless, thoughts of suicide clutter my mind
Rejection, self-hate enter my soul
My heart is left with a gigantic hole
Why did you violate me?
Is this the way my life is destined to be?
I don't understand

CHAPTER 3

Ain't No Sunshine

From the outside looking in, Pam's relationship with her aunt/ mother was picture perfect. She and Diane attended church. They wore the right clothes with the right shoes, hat, purse and accessories to match. They had the right hairstyles. They knew all the right people. Diane never allowed Pam to choose just any color or style for herself; she only took Pam along for measurement purposes.

A day at the mall was just that: from sunup to sundown, Diane dragged Pam around in and out of the stores. Pam longed for closeness with Diane like other girls seemed to have with their mothers. However, their shopping trips were never a time for bonding. Rather, everything was rushed and the time was filled with complaints and murmuring. Diane never took the initiative to get acquainted with Pam or to discover any common interests or traits. Diane actually considered her an ungrateful girl who had no sense of fashion, only tasteless style. Diane was all about maintaining an image and only an image.

Diane was very involved at her church. She was a missionary, a stewardess, a deaconess, a member of the prayer and bible band, a mother of the church, president of several auxiliaries and occasionally taught Sunday school. So, she felt she was just going to church to offer support to all of the "baby" Christians there, because she always felt she already had everything together. Diane refused to believe that any of the lessons preached across the pulpit were for her. After all, they addressed the "average" Christian. She felt she didn't have any issues because she never drank alcohol, tried drugs, had sex with a man other than her husband, or engaged in any of the other dreadful sins that others members testified receiving deliverance from. Even though she did smoke cigarettes, she did not feel that was a reason for her to change.

Diane believed in God, but she felt that the ordinary person with "issues," especially someone in her family or someone she knew personally, could never be used by Him. She had no problem verbalizing her opinion either, no matter how cruel or inappropriate her delivery was.

Diane was particularly pleasant to the pastor and his family, incredibly so, often cooking elaborate dinners and desserts for them. Her generosity made it hard to confront her about her character flaws. She could change like a chameleon, being delightfully charming with fellow members one minute and then suddenly being ill-tempered as soon as the car left the church parking lot.

Pam enjoyed going to church. It served as a safe haven for her. She was an active member in the youth department and often went on field trips. Diane made sure Pam's entire extra-curricular environment provided social etiquette. Meanwhile, Otis refused to join the church. Instead, he joined a motorcycle club and ran numbers at the bookie joint.

Otis had a volatile and domineering relationship with Pam. He abused her physically, mentally and emotionally, and sexually molested her repeatedly from the age of five until she was fifteen. For instance, on more than one occasion, while Diane would cook dinner and without her knowledge, Otis would command Pam to stand in the hallway and expose herself to him as he strategically sat at the kitchen table where he could have a clear view down the hall and covertly masturbate. His instructions were concise and very intimidating. He made her stand there after she had gotten out of the shower, disrobe and expose her young naked body. She was directed to do this before going to her room to dress.

Often, too, Otis insisted on being alone with Pam at home, always promising to take her to a picture show while Diane went out shopping or was working overtime. While she was gone, he would make Pam perform sexual favors, like have her look at money and body soap with pictures of naked women on them while he masturbated or rubbed his penis on her leg. One time when Pam and Otis were in a heated argument, Pam mustered up the courage to confront him in front of Diane about all the abuse. He flat-out denied abusing her in any way, and then Diane ridiculed and badgered her with a stream of rhetorical questions that she never gave Pam an opportunity to answer. She called Pam a liar, among other things. Diane always defended Otis, even saying at one point, "Regardless of what he did, he was a good man, and he did a lot of good things."

Diane was a person who lived in a constant state of denial about any personal struggles or issues. Point blank, she was in denial of the truth. She lived in her own world where she compartmentalized everything in her mind, never allowing herself any space or time to deal with her pain. Therefore, her heartache was never addressed. It's hard to say or even assume what happened to her to make her so jaded and bitter. What was for sure is that Diane could just mentally remove herself and any emotions from the situation.

Diane also abused Pam mentally, physically and emotionally. She constantly threw things up in Pam's face to make her feel like she was forever indebted to her, like, "Your mother didn't want you" and that Myrtle had a problem with promiscuity and alcohol and Pam was going to be just like her. Diane would go on and on telling Pam horrible things about her mother, who birthed eleven children (nine boys and two girls). "There were plenty of people who wanted children and couldn't have them," and "Why did God give her all those kids when she didn't teach or show them anything?" and "Myrtle didn't deserve to have all those kids." Diane even ridiculed Pam about her name. Myrtle named her after her and Diane's mother, and Diane didn't like that at all. She often told Pam she wasn't worthy to have that name.

Both Diane and Otis felt that Pam was very ungrateful. After all, Otis gave Pam any material possession she desired, from the latest fashionable clothes to a 1967 Falcon, but this was to cover up his guilt. Still, he felt like he owned her and that he could do anything to her. He didn't even care about leaving bruises on her, either. He would sock her in the face, grab her by the neck, violently choke her, and slap her with an open hand without any remorse. Even that time he gave her a black eye.

Otis had no fear of the authorities. He even took Pam directly to the police station and dared her to tell the police anything that had transpired. During the 1950s and 1960s, the authorities did not consider it out of the ordinary for a child to have a bruise or black eye. They only told her, "Next time, do what you're told to do."

Pam felt alone. So, you can imagine how elated she was when her older brother Patrick started writing her letters. Apparently, Patrick lied about his age and joined the Marines to help support his family at the tender age of sixteen. In his letters, he told her about her other brothers and her mother and father. Pam had no idea who her parents were. Fortunately, Diane was very much aware of the ongoing communication between Pam and her brother and approved of it.

In fact, when Patrick graduated from boot camp, it was Diane who took Pam to the ceremony at Camp Pendleton in Oceanside, California. Patrick's first assignment was as a radioman in the Vietnam War. His primary duty was to run and signal for help in case of an emergency. He was assigned that job because he could outrun his squad. Pam and Patrick continued to write each other, and they became extremely close. Patrick gave her their mother's address in one of his letters, and soon Pam began writing Myrtle. Diane was oblivious to this and would not have been in agreement with it.

It wasn't before long, however, that Pam's and Patrick's letters got intercepted by Otis, who began stealing them and throwing them away. Pam was so heartbroken and couldn't take the abuse anymore. She started rebelling in any way she could just so she didn't have to be in that house. She longed to live with her mother and siblings and often asked to be sent to Cleveland. It was her lifelong dream to be together with her real family. But Otis and Diane told her that would never be an option.

Empty Soul

Filled with despondency, thoughts of desolation
Joy is lost, therefore I have no consideration
My soul is hollow
Dreams implore me to dare
Fearless youth without a care
Have my own values and a firm belief
I'll shout it out
To the world without being discreet
Empty soul trying to find my way
How come you won't listen to what I have to say?
Are you afraid of what you might learn?
No heart of compassion, in your rudeness you reply,
"It's simply not my concern."
But it is – for you see, I'm the future seed
Through me your vision lives
OH, YES, INDEED!
My pride has been crushed, yet my strength lives
It's vital, detrimental, I haven't figured out that part, but
I know it's instrumental to watch, know, learn and love me
Whisper in my ear when I'm hurting; I can be
All that I do and don't say . . . Hey!
Listen! Please! So you can understand what is going on deep within
Sometimes I don't need reprimanding; I desire a close friend
Fear overwhelms me from walking in my truth
You insist on depositing negative words into my spirit?
The mental chatter still torments my soul. Yes, I still hear it.
You considered it fun to manipulate my mind
It's only in a crowded room when people are watching; you are kind
Please leave me alone

I desire to be free
You see
I have determination despite what you might say
God recognizes my voice and He hears me when I pray
The joy, the laughter, the pain and the grief
I know He is watching as you mock and laugh at me in your own
disbelief
My spirit knows the truth
My tears flow like a strong river's current
so deep
Oh, God, where are You?

CHAPTER 4

Shattered Dreams

T hough Otis terminated Pam's channel of communication with Patrick, she did have one other person she could talk to: her Aunt Regina. Regina was Diane's younger sister. She lived nearby and had a daughter named Desiree, or as family referred to her, "Desi." Pam was ten years older than her, but they had a unique bond, like sisters. Regina's house was a place of refuge for Pam, like the church. It was a place she could relax, get peace of mind and just plain be a kid.

Pam enjoyed spending time with Regina and Desiree because she felt wanted, loved and connected. As a single parent who worked the graveyard shift as a hospital nurse's aide, Regina didn't have as much money as Otis and Diane did, but she loved Pam unconditionally and treated her like she was her very own daughter. She would watch cartoons with Pam and Desi and do art projects with them, like painting figurines and sewing bed pillows with dolls' patterns. She would take the girls to the park and afterward make cookies and treats, and she often chaperoned them to their Girl Scouts activities. It gave Pam the opportunity to be out of Diane's and Otis' house and spend the night there.

Although Regina was aware that some things weren't quite right in Diane and Otis's home, she was non-confrontational. She never challenged either one of them about their methods of discipline nor questioned them about Pam's accusations of the sexual, mental and physical abuse. What she did do was provide a safe and loving environment. Her door was always open, and she was someone Pam could always go to.

Initially, Diane and Otis were okay with Pam spending time with Regina and Desiree. But then Diane started having a problem with their close-knit relationship. As Pam spent more time at their house, Diane grew suspicious, feeling as though Regina was trying to take her place. Diane started perceiving her as a threat.

On one occasion, for no apparent reason, Otis and Diane went to Regina's house yelling and screaming, demanding that she open the door. When Regina finally did, Pam got a severe beating. Otis first beat her all the way from Regina's front door to the car and then continued with a follow-up beating once they arrived home. Diane couldn't understand why Pam enjoyed going to Regina's house in light of the fact that Regina was an unwed mother who lived in the projects. Diane was unable to see Regina's genuine ability to connect with and love children.

Pam began to rebel openly against Otis's harsh means of discipline, vocally questioning him during the beatings. She demanded to know why he slapped her with an open hand across the face with so much force that her frail body fell to the floor, or why he threw her across the room right after violently choking her. To escape this vicious cycle of abuse, Pam frequently ran away and slept over a few of her girlfriends' houses. A temporary fix. She was running out of places to go.

Ultimately, Diane and Otis begrudgingly gave in and, in the summer of 1968, at the age of fourteen, Pam was sent to live with her mother Myrtle and eight brothers (Patrick was still serving in the Marines, and her sister Wanda had not been born yet). The ride to the airport was one of many heart-wrenching experiences. Diane and Otis were very distraught, and Otis gave Pam his Mason ring on a chain and placed it around her neck. He had loaded twelve labeled boxes containing her clothes, shoes, records, record player and other prized possessions. Diane had cried the entire way there and even followed Pam on the airplane and begged her not to leave.

Pam was crying as well. As dysfunctional as Diane and Otis were, they were the only parents she knew. At the same time, in her heart she wanted to know. She had to know for herself who her real mother was. Why did Diane, Otis and other family members hate this woman so much and talk about her so badly? She had to see this woman face-to-face. Finally, she was going to see for herself the woman she yearned to know: her birth mother.

Once Pam arrived in Cleveland, her lifelong dream of being reunited with her real family soon became a living nightmare. She was immediately introduced to stark poverty—something she knew absolutely nothing about. Myrtle and Pam's eight brothers, all of them younger than her and born between two and four years apart, lived in a filthy, roach-infested, three-room shack. Upon entering, the first room was a living room/bedroom where seven brothers slept. Myrtle had converted it to serve as a multi-purpose room. There was a set of bunk beds in the middle of the floor and in the corner was a couch where guests sat. The next room Pam shared with Myrtle and Pam's youngest brother Cameron, who was only two months old. The last room was the kitchen/bathroom.

Pam wasn't used to living in these conditions. The entire environment was a culture shock. At her aunt and uncle's house, she had her own room, with all the amenities she desired. She didn't have to share anything with Otis, Jr., as he also had his own room with the same luxuries. At Myrtle's, soon enough Pam's brothers destroyed all of her prized possessions: her records, television and record player. It was apparent they were jealous of this long-lost sister who seemed to have lived a very privileged life. They never had things of their own, so they had no concept of how to take care of or appreciate other people's belongings. The relationship between Pam, her brothers and her mother proved very complicated due to all of the contributing factors. She talked, acted and carried herself differently. She was an outsider entering their domain. From what they could see, she thought she was better than them.

Myrtle didn't have a work history, and she received public assistance. This concept was foreign to Pam because Diane and Otis went to work every day. Myrtle constantly struggled to make ends meet, being a single mother who cared for her children alone. Since she was on a fixed income, clothing and shoes ran out quickly, as did even the bare necessities like soap, toilet paper and toothpaste.

The food supply was always very limited or non-existent, so Pam's brothers had to help support the family as best they could. Patrick sent money from Vietnam. Peter got a job at the grocery store. Darrell, who was two years younger than Pam, worked as a caddy at the neighborhood golfing club. Bruce and Jack were not old enough to have regular jobs, so they stole food like bread and lunchmeat from the grocery store. The last three siblings, Derrick, Brian and Cameron, were too young to contribute to the household.

It didn't take long for Myrtle to coerce Pam to tag along with Bruce and Jack to steal food. She would just sternly insist, "Whatever you steal, be sure not to get caught." As a result, Bruce and Jack spent most of their childhood and adolescent years in juvenile halls, detention centers and boys' homes. The boys were also obligated to support Myrtle's cigarette and beer habits.

Since Myrtle enjoyed the party life, she spent most of her time at a nightclub or bar. This was another culture shock to Pam, as she was never exposed to adults drinking or going out to a nightclub on a regular basis. Myrtle wore all of Pam's clothes to the local bar, and also assigned her the duty of being her personal hairdresser. Myrtle would call Pam all sorts of profane names if she didn't fix her hair just the way she liked it.

Myrtle didn't just cuss out Pam or her children. She cussed out anyone in a heartbeat, and spared no feelings. She was an angry and bitter person. She found it difficult to display affection toward her children. She also had little to no contact with their fathers. After she divorced Stanley, she gave birth to Darrell, Bruce and Jack, whose father was a married man named Willie D. Willie D. was semi-involved in the boys' life—until his wife shot him dead on the railroad tracks. Myrtle then had Derrick, Brian and Cameron by another married man, Frankie Joe, whose wife limited his participation in his sons' lives.

Under such dysfunction, it wasn't long before Pam and her brothers each ventured out on their own respective quests to find some form of attention. Sadly, the consequences manifested through drugs, drinking, jail, death and premature parenting. All of Myrtle's children except Pam's youngest brother Cameron went this route. All this harsh reality was not what Pam expected at all.

Pam only saw her father Stanley on occasion. He had remarried, and Myrtle gave Pam an ultimatum that it be either his new family and Myrtle's family, but not both. Stanley did give Pam money whenever she needed anything for school or just for pocket money. Once, he had given her fifty dollars for school shoes, but as soon as Myrtle found out, she took it, telling Pam fifty dollars was too much for school shoes, then taking her to a secondhand store to buy a pair of shoes for fifteen dollars and keeping the remaining thirty-five dollars for herself. Pam had never been to a secondhand store. She didn't even know they existed, since Diane only shopped at major department stores.

On another occasion, Pam and Myrtle walked five miles in the snow to Frankie Joe's house for money, as they had no food at home. Pam was elated because at Frankie Joe's house, they ate fried apples every day. When they arrived, Myrtle made Pam go up to the house and knock on the door. Frankie Joe's wife did not invite Pam in out of the cold but insisted she stay on the porch. "One of Myrtle's illegitimate children is standing outside," she yelled out to Frankie Joe. When he came to the door, he offered neither a smile nor a seat inside. He gave Pam five dollars and turned to walk away. Pam was pretty shocked! "Five dollars?! That's it?!" she blurted out. Frankie Joe immediately turned around and slapped her. She couldn't wait to get back to tell her mother what he did. But, instead of comforting Pam or defending her, Myrtle accused her of provoking him.

The nightmare only continued to unfold for Pam. To bring in more money, Myrtle cajoled her into prostitution. She insisted Pam befriend a teenage girl in the neighborhood named Suga' Pie, who was extremely promiscuous and already had a baby, so, to make ends meet, she would "turn tricks." Pam's assignment was to accompany Suga' Pie on these exploits to learn the ropes. Myrtle persuaded Pam to have relations with older men in exchange for money, cigarettes and beer, and she made it emphatically clear that Pam was to return all earnings directly to her.

Outside of all this confusion, Pam did find solitude at her grandparents' house, which was nearby. Myrtle's father Timothy and stepmother Grace adored Pam, and she felt safe with them. It was just like being with Regina and Desiree. She often went to church with Grace and even got saved and baptized. But, sadly, whenever her grandparents dropped her back home to Myrtle's house, the mental abuse resumed. For instance, Myrtle tried to turn Pam's brothers against her. Pam eventually found her escape from reality though drinking and smoking marijuana with her brothers and skipping school.

As if bad could not get worse, Myrtle was ordered to remove her family from the shack. A Health Department inspector came out and condemned the grounds for unsafe conditions and vermin. Myrtle had no money and no place to stay. Thankfully, Otis's cousin Louise lived nearby in a two-story house and allowed Myrtle, Pam and her brothers to live with them temporarily. There was one bedroom downstairs, which was Louise's bedroom, and two upstairs, one for the boys and the other for Myrtle, Pam and Cameron.

Shortly after they moved in, Louise suddenly became ill and died. Myrtle and her children stayed in the home until they could move into a housing project the following summer, in 1969.

Meanwhile, Timothy and Grace continued to be actively involved in Pam's life, especially when Myrtle's living conditions became unstable. Pam was so grateful because her grandparents spent time with her and showed her love during a time that her mind was full of confusion and despair. In her heart, she wanted get to know her mother and brothers and desired a close relationship with them. After all, this was why she wanted to move to Cleveland in the first place.

Timothy became aware of some of what was going on with Pam, as rumors were circulating around town. He questioned her about it and she confirmed the rumors were true. He then called Diane and Otis to inform them, urging them to step in immediately because reform school was the next option due to her truancies.

Diane and Pam communicated through her grandparents, with Pam being very forthcoming about everything. Diane purchased a plane ticket for her to return to California and instructed her to leave with the clothes on her back and to go straight to the airport. Pam felt she was betraying her mother and brothers by leaving, but she was not happy there. Honestly, though, she wasn't happy in California either.

The next evening, Timothy came by the house and slipped Pam fifty dollars for cab fare to the airport. Pam slept with the fifty dollars in her undergarments all night. She feared that Myrtle would take it like she had done before. The next day, as a decoy, Pam said she was going to go with Suga' Pie to the mall. The bus had gotten about a half-mile down the street when Pam rang the bell to get off at the next stop. From there, she caught a cab to the airport and boarded the plane back to California. She didn't say goodbye to her brothers or Myrtle. She didn't speak to any of them again until five years later, when she was pregnant with Seanette. By that time, Myrtle had another baby by Frankie Joe. This time, it was a girl, Wanda. She was Myrtle's last child.

Who is My Mother?

I long for her touch like an infant who cries
in the midnight to be held.
Where are you? It's dark in this hole.
Dreams of you holding me in your arms as you whisper,
"I love you," before you tuck me in the bed and say goodnight.
No made-up book story,
This here reality of mine is a daily nightmare.
I fight for you to notice me, for your love or
A few words to show me you care.
You offer only condescending comments and hideous stares.
Why do you hate me?
I promise, I don't feel I'm better than you.
For years, I dreamt of this moment, this time . . . My real family
—that's all I've been on a search to find.
These words I speak to you are true.
. . . I love you, truly I do

CHAPTER 5

Runaway Child Running Wild

In the late summer of 1969, Pam arrived back in California with Otis and Diane. The physical, mental and sexual abuse not only resumed but escalated. Pam found no refuge and lasted only about one month before she left to stay with Regina and Desiree for a while. By this time, Otis, Jr., was no longer living in the home, either. Otis had coerced Diane to admit their son for an extended stay in a state mental hospital, for shock treatments and further evaluation.

Regina helped Pam acquire emancipation, which was relatively easy since Diane and Otis had never pursued legal guardianship of her. All that was required for her freedom was a simple notarized letter from Myrtle proving that she was, in fact, Pam's biological mother, which Myrtle agreed to provide.

Pam stayed with friends while she waited for her mother's letter to arrive at Regina's house. Once it came, Pam went to the police station to request an escort at Otis' and Diane's house so she could retrieve her belongings. The police drove her there and when they approached the door, Otis met them and thanked them for returning "their" daughter home. The police then showed Otis and Diane Myrtle's letter. Diane began to question Pam on why she brought the police to their home. Pam then openly asked Otis to confess to molesting her, and Otis again denied it ever happened. Diane never asked Pam for her side of the story. Once again, she sided with her husband and degraded Pam with derogatory insults. But Pam didn't care. She was just happy to leave their house, and her communication with them from this point was non-existent for the next several years.

Pam initially moved in with a childhood friend, named Lisa, and her mother and she continued to attend high school and also started working to pay for room and board. Later, she enrolled in an onsite surgical technician program at a local vocational school. She developed close relationships with other young women over the next two or three years. One of them became a lifelong friend whose family became like a second family to Pam. Her name was Joy and she would have a significant impact on the daughter Pam would have in the coming years.

Two other close relationships were with two fellow vocational school students. Debbie would become Pam's roommate as well as her future drug dealer; and a young man named Sean would become Pam's future child's father. Both Debbie and Sean drank and smoked weed, which became the common bond among the three of them.

A runaway like Pam and forsaken by his family, Sean Cannon III was originally from New Mexico, where he and his twelve brothers and sisters grew up in poverty. His father, Sean, Sr., was a Pentecostal minister, and his mother, Ellie, was a full-blooded Native American. Sean, Sr. was a stern man and was physically abusive like Otis, while Ellie was a passive woman who, unlike Diane, never got "out of line." She didn't defend herself or her children in hopes that Sean, Sr. would stop the physical abuse on his own. That never happened.

Ellie never seriously considered leaving her husband. Sean Cannon, Sr. was a well-known minister in the community. She feared him and, most of all, she feared being alone with thirteen children. Ellie left the Indian reservation to be with Sean, Sr., and there was no family to return to. He was her first love and repeatedly told her that she was incapable of being or doing anything without him, and she believed him. Sadly, it eventually cost Ellie her life. She sustained a head blow by him and remained in a coma until he gave the hospital permission to take her off life support.

Sean, Sr. despised Sean from birth because he believed his namesake was the result of Ellie cheating on him. With some of their children already grown, they had lost a baby, Sean Cannon II, shortly before she got pregnant with Sean III. Even though Sean was the spitting image of his father, his father thought it was impossible for Ellie to conceive so soon after the death of Sean II. As a result, Sean always referred to himself as the child out of wedlock.

Sean, Sr. was firm with all his children, but he was incredibly cruel toward Sean. He would beat him for no reason, lock him in a closet or even outside the home, while all the children were inside. The rule was that, if the other kids were caught talking or playing with Sean, they were shunned right along with him.

There were only three family members Sean developed a close bond with: his older sisters Eartha and Helen, and older cousin Rachel. Rachel's house was the only place of refuge for Sean. Still, the love of these family members wasn't enough for him. When he was thirteen years old and Helen was eighteen, they ran away from home. They earned their keep on the streets by tagging along with pimps, prostitutes, thugs and street hustlers. They got a crash course in street life and soon were committing every crime imaginable together. Eventually, they hitchhiked from New Mexico and settled in California. There, they started experimenting with drugs like acid tabs, pills (uppers and downers), weed, PCP, alcohol and crack cocaine. Eventually, Helen became a homeless heroin addict and Sean became an alcoholic and a crack abuser.

Pam and Sean were dating exclusively by the time she graduated from the vocational school, although he didn't graduate from the horticulture program he was enrolled in. She landed a job in the Wilshire District as a surgical technician, and he resorted back to his former means of earning a living: scamming people and selling drugs. At this point, Pam got back in contact with her close friend Joy and spent lots of time with her at her apartment in Los Angeles. On the weekends when Pam was not working, she and Sean spent time with Joy, her nine brothers and sisters, and especially her mother, Sonia. Sonia was a humble woman. She was the total opposite of any mother figure in Pam's life up to that point. Pam not only trusted Sonia but valued her opinion.

Pam's life seemed to be looking up. She had a mother figure in Sonia, who loved and treated her as her very own, she had nine "brothers and sisters" she considered family, and she had a boyfriend who appeared to adore her.

Pam was pregnant for five whole months before she realized it. That's when Sean's "loving" ways began to turn more possessive and abusive, leading Pam to seek refuge in Sonia. She would cry and tell Sonia all the horrible things Sean did to her, such as the time during the pregnancy that Sean held her down on the bed and threatened to stick her in the eye with a sewing needle. On another occasion, he swung a telephone receiver towards her stomach and threatened to kill her unborn child if she ever tried to leave him.

One way or another, Diane and Otis caught wind of Pam's whereabouts and contacted Sonia. Sonia informed them that Pam was pregnant. She then persuaded Pam to contact them. Initially, Diane and Otis were not supportive. They were furious with Pam because they felt she had ruined her life. But after the smoke cleared, they came to Sonia's house to see her and periodically gave her money.

As Pam continued to work as a surgical technician, Sean continued to perfect his street game. He had become what would be called a jack-of-all-trades. He was a serious con artist who could change his accent from his native New Mexican accent to Southern, Jamaican, even Australian. You name it; Sean could do it! He also spoke Spanish fluently. He had the ability to change his demeanor on demand anytime, anyplace and anywhere. He was so good at manipulating people, it became a game for him to see how he could get over on them. Pam disliked this trait the most about him. Aside from it being wrong, she had a hard time keeping up with his different schemes and the different personalities that came with them. Still, she played the part of the loving, compliant girlfriend while she worked on a back-up plan. She learned how to "jump into character" from watching him.

As the days, weeks and months went by, it became more apparent to Pam that she had to get away from Sean. She wanted to start her life all over again. She wanted her child to have a better life than the one Sean was providing. So, once her daughter was born, Pam called Diane and Otis. It was the last place she wanted to go, given the history, but she felt her options had run out. She knew if Sean insisted on being in her and her child's life, he would be forced to behave himself at their house. Diane and Otis agreed to let Pam move in, but first they wanted to meet with her and Sean. Sean presented himself as a hard-working, self-employed man, attempting to sell them the same dream he sold to Pam. Frankly, Diane wasn't impressed. She saw right through all of his fast-talking nonsense. In any event, she had a laundry list of rules for both Pam and Sean to abide by, and they both agreed.

Conversely, Otis, to Pam's surprise, was very nice. After they moved in, he gave Pam whatever she needed or wanted. She knew he felt guilty about all the abuse he subjected her to when she was younger. He even co-signed on a Volkswagen for her, which infuriated Diane! She couldn't understand why he was so generous and just assumed that Pam had him wrapped around her finger. Only Otis and Pam knew what the real motive was. Still, Diane did convert the spare room into a nursery, and she even took a six-week leave from her job to help Pam take care of the baby.

By the time the baby was born, Sean's and Pam's relationship was on the rocks. Pam focused all her time and energy on her new daughter, whom she named Seanette. She didn't care about Sean and his empty promises or Diane's and Otis's condescending comments, which had continued in spite of some improvement since she moved back in. Pam was happy that her daughter's entry into the world was here, and she prayed and made a vow to the Lord that she would raise Seanette to know Him. In the meantime, she did her best to settle in and continued to work in the nursing field.

Sean himself even got a job at the local warehouse, but that was short-lived. Soon, he started taking the car and hanging out in Los Angeles, accepting no responsibility as a father or a mate. Seriously, his "change" lasted about as long as that warehouse job and, inevitably, he reverted to his old self. When Pam tried to confront him, he resorted to his usual violent outbursts. During one of their heated arguments, Diane came home from work and heard the commotion. She immediately went to the locked gun cabinet, retrieved a shotgun, walked down the hallway and opened their bedroom door. She entered the room and calmly told Sean he had a choice: either he could leave voluntarily, or the Los Angeles County Coroner would carry him out. Sean selected the first option.

With Sean gone, Pam found some happiness being back on her old stomping grounds. By this time, her dear friend Regina had landed a part-time job as an aide at the local children's center. She also had another baby after Desiree, a girl she named Angel. Angel was eighteen months older than Pam's daughter, and Desiree was ten years older. Soon, all three of them—Desiree, Angel and Seanette—were inseparable, like sisters. Seanette spent her early infant and childhood years with Regina and her girls. Regina's house would become a safe haven for her, just like it had been for Pam.

Pam continued to work. She soon caught up with some of her high school friends who also had children. She and Sean also began to communicate again and, like always, he promised to change. At first, Pam did a few trial runs with him by herself. She would drop Seanette off at Regina's house on a late Friday night after Desiree and Angel were asleep, and return Sunday evening. Regina never turned Pam away; and she always took Seanette in.

Pam half-heartedly believed all of Sean's promises to change. Before long, he talked her into moving back to Los Angeles. Her motivation was to show Diane and Otis that she could be self-sufficient and that she could take care of her child alone. As odd as it seemed in light of her history with them, she still always wanted to make them proud. She and Sean found an apartment in Los Angeles, near Arlington Avenue and Washington Boulevard. Unfortunately, like always, Sean's temper began to flare up again and the physical altercations resurfaced.

Pam realized moving out Otis' and Diane's house was a big mistake. The fantasy she had of her, Sean and Seanette making it as a family quickly faded. Nothing but the location had changed. No matter how hard she tried to grant Sean's every wish like a genie, he always found something wrong. The more she tried to please him, the less he was satisfied. If she cleaned the apartment, he still complained about how filthy it was. If she gave him a glass of water, he claimed it wasn't cold enough. Sean treated Pam as his slave.

He never got a job as he promised and continued to use drugs, hustle and take advantage of others to make quick money. Then one day, Sean went to go visit his family in New Mexico. Pam knew time was of the essence.

Mother's Cry

Mother's cry baby don't know why
Her tears, so deep, so true
Mother's cry baby don't know why she
is sad, lonely and blue
Mother's cry baby don't understand
Momma's face is bruised by the hands of her man
Mother's cry the sacrifice she provides for her future seed
Mother's cry she abandons self-love to unconditionally
supply every need
Mother's cry the baby cries as
She medicates her hurts through different highs
Mother's cry exhausted she sighs
She keeps the faith and prays for a better tomorrow
Mother's cry desperately she tries
to let go of her present sorrow
Baby sighs, "Momma, please tell me, why do you cry?"

CHAPTER 6

On a Wing and a Prayer

Pam abandoned Sean's apartment with two-year-old Seanette in her arms and only a suitcase filled with her and Seanette's clothes. She left without all the furniture, pictures and memories, both good and bad. It was one of many unsuccessful attempts to get away from Sean. She laid low for two weeks and spent time with different friends and Regina. Eventually, she called Diane and Otis, and they moved her into another apartment on the west side of Los Angeles.

Diane helped Pam decorate and furnish her new place and even made curtains for the windows. Pam soon settled in and met Kaneatra, who lived in the apartment building next door. They both had some things in common. For instance, Kaneatra, like Pam, was in the nursing profession. She was also in a very abusive relationship. It wasn't long before they became good friends. Like Pam's dear friend Joy, Kaneatra became an aunt to Seanette, and her three children were like Seanette's cousins. Audrey, Oliver and Tina were all older than Seanette, and while Pam was working, Seanette spent a lot of time them.

One day, Pam heard a knock at the door. She was startled when she looked through the peephole and saw Sean standing there. Apparently, he had gone to the post office and, just like that, he had the new address. He had come there before and Kaneatra saw him. She attempted to lie, denying that Pam lived there. But Sean camped out in front of the apartment building until he saw Pam and Seanette.

At first, Sean pounded on the door demanding to see Seanette. Then, he started sobbing, begging and pleading for Pam to open the door. That made her feel bad, so she let him in. Sean began yelling and screaming and accusing her of taking his daughter away from him. The truth of the matter was, Sean didn't know what to do. He told her he realized she was no longer afraid of him, and that surprised him. She had built up the courage to leave him, and he realized his intimidation tactics were ineffective. Pam only half-heartedly believed Sean, but she gave him another chance anyway.

Unfortunately, this honeymoon period was shorter than the last time. Sean became more and more possessive as the days went by, as did his drug and alcohol intake and his erratic behavior. Some days, he was charming and thoughtful, promising to change and be a responsible father and loving boyfriend. On other days, he was a monster.

Pam made yet another escape from Sean. Like she did the last time, she left everything in the apartment (pictures, clothes, furniture and, most of all, memories) and moved to the east side of Los Angeles with her second family, Joy and her sisters and brothers, although their mother Sonia had become ill and passed away. During this time, Pam also reunited with Debbie. Every day that she was away from Sean, she grew stronger mentally and emotionally. She saved her money and moved in an apartment back on the west side.

Then one day, when Pam's babysitter was at the apartment to look after Seanette while Pam went to work, Sean showed up. Again, he was able to find out where she was. This time when he came, he kicked in the door and kidnapped Seanette. Pam was livid when she returned from work. Immediately, she asked Debbie to give her a ride over to Sean's house, and she asked two male friends to go over there, kick the door in and take Seanette. When Pam arrived at Sean's apartment, his older sister Helen was there alone with Seanette. Helen said she didn't want any problems and readily handed Seanette over. Sean was furious when he returned and retaliated by sending the police to Debbie's house. They took temporary custody of Seanette, but she was later released back to her mother that night.

Pam and Sean then fought things out in a huge custody battle. Despite the lies Sean tried to paint against Pam's character, the judge ruled in her favor. It was finally over! Pam had concrete protection, THE LAW! The court awarded Sean visitation rights for every other weekend, Wednesdays overnight and Thursday afternoons. He was allowed to pick Seanette up from school and return her to Pam. Sean respected the law. For now.

My World

Alone I sit in my room with my imaginary friend,
who resides in my pocket
His illuminating charisma
Is like a lamp surging energy from a wall socket
You take nothing from me
You genuinely enjoy my company
I am the perfect hostess as I hope this monologue will never fade
I invite you to sit down at the kitchen table
We laugh and talk and enjoy the cookies and
warm tea that I made.

CHAPTER 7
Clear Skies, Rainbows and Sunshine

During the late 1970s and early 1980s, Seanette went through many transitions that happened simultaneously. The memories she retained were of a rather broad yet confusing spectrum.

They ranged from her feeling extremely secure, safe and happy, to feeling lonely, despondent and destitute. She enjoyed spending time with both of her parents, her grandparents and other family and loved ones who adopted her as niece, sister or cousin. But, there were also traumatic events brought on by some of those she had grown to love.

As a child, Seanette was very petite. Pam and Diane always dressed her in beautiful dresses with ruffles, and they made certain she had proper etiquette in fashion, appearance and poise. She resembled a Victorian princess. Although Pam didn't attend church regularly, she often sent Seanette with "Auntie" Joy. After her mother Sonia died, Joy turned her life completely around, including becoming a born-again Christian. At barely twenty-five years of age, she also took on the responsibility of caring for all of her younger siblings. Joy was a God-sent angel who helped keep Seanette grounded in Christ.

Joy took her younger siblings, Seanette and whoever else could fit to church. Seanette enjoyed going to church. She enjoyed participating in choir rehearsal, youth group, Sunday school and Bible study. She was fond of going to the teen group with "Auntie" Janet and "Uncle" Jermaine, Joy's teenage sister and her boyfriend. Even though Seanette was only five years old, they never treated her like she was a baby. She adored being around them. During church services, Jermaine regularly cracked jokes, mimicking the pastor and other church members. He kept everyone laughing all the time. Joy tried to reprimand him, but she couldn't keep a straight face herself! He was genuinely hilarious! Janet treated Seanette like she was her real niece. She combed her hair and dressed her in all the latest styles for church.

During one evening service, when the pastor extended the altar call, Seanette noticed a tugging at her heart and she immediately felt an overwhelming presence of love, joy and peace. She responded with the conscious decision to walk down the church aisle. When she approached the altar, the pastor took her hand and, with loving eyes, asked her what she wanted. He lowered the microphone from his mouth so the whole congregation could hear. She stated as clear as day, "I want to be saved and for Jesus to come into my heart and be my friend." Seanette was five years old. Not long after that evening, she was baptized and Pam, Diane and Joy were all there.

Education and God were top priorities to Pam for Seanette. Even though at home Pam lived the polar opposite of what a Christian life should have been, she always stressed to Seanette the importance of school and having a relationship with Jesus.

By this time, Pam and Seanette had moved yet again, this time to an apartment in the Leimert Park community of Los Angeles, which was at that time considered a middle-class area for African-American families. Unfortunately, Sean still harassed Pam for a few years, ignoring a court order and showing up wherever they were. At the new apartment, he would regularly break the front door or side window with his fist, come in and pull Pam outside by her nightgown, all in front of Seanette. Pam constantly called the police on him, but he always fled the scene before they arrived. Seanette would often cry because she wanted to go with him.

Despite Sean's bullying, manipulation and control tactics, Pam never returned to him. She and Seanette loved their apartment and neighborhood because it was finally home to them, and Pam did a fantastic job decorating it and keeping it immaculate. She even had custom-made drapes with shades and the latest furniture to match in every room.

Like the rest of their home, Seanette's bedroom was spotless. Pam was very strict about Seanette keeping her room orderly at all times, or else! Since she was an only child, her room was the average child's fantasy, with every toy and gadget imaginable. Pam and Diane, and even sometimes Sean, made sure of it. She had stuffed animals and a complete toy kitchen set, fully loaded with a stove, refrigerator and sink. She also had a two-story dollhouse with all the furniture. She could paint, read books and play board and card games (by herself), and she enjoyed brainteaser activities such as crosswords and puzzles.

Seanette took very good care of all her belongings, and everything was in mint condition. In each drawer, all of her clothes were neatly arranged and folded. In her closet, her shoes were always perfectly lined up and school uniforms neatly hung, freshly pressed from the cleaners. Her shoes and clothing were itemized into three categories — school, play and church — and nothing was ever out of place. Pam allowed Seanette to have company in her room, but it had to be cleaned and returned to its original pristine condition after company left.

Pam enrolled Seanette into Hillcrest, a prestigious private parochial school nearby. She attended Hillcrest for four consecutive years, from kindergarten through third grade. She was popular among all her classmates, and since it was a small school, she grew up with the same kids and attended all their birthday parties.

Besides the church, Hillcrest offered the only real stability Seanette had in her life. In kindergarten, she formed a healthy relationship with a friend named Dominic that lasted until the third grade. They had a major crush on each other and ate lunch together every day. Dominic's mother always made him hamburgers drowned in mustard on white bread. He was so courteous; he offered her some every day. They named each other after their favorite ice cream flavors; he called her "Mint Chip" and she called him "Chocolate Chip."

Seanette also established a close friendship with a girl named Stacy, who lived with her parents in the apartment building next door. Seanette and Stacy usually occupied themselves with riding their Big

Wheels through the neighborhood, asking their friendly mailman, Tom, all kinds of "mail questions," and making mud pies all day long. Stacy was easygoing and genuinely liked Seanette. The girls had a lot of things in common. They were both only children, so they were both spoiled. She had just as many toys, and she enjoyed sharing. She was never jealous of Seanette, so she didn't mistreat or take advantage of her.

Stacy and Seanette were inseparable. They always played together and even had their birthday parties at the same places. The local burger joint had an arcade filled with games and characters who dressed up, and you could have your picture taken. Seanette really liked the pizza parlor because they had big slices of pizza, all she could eat.

Unwanted Affection

Secretive violation
No consideration
of the age or background
I'm confused with this obsession
You have found with me
I didn't ask for this kind of attention
How many times do I have to mention?
I just want to play
I don't like this game
You try to persuade me
To make me stay
I was never taught how to say
I don't like it
or that it's not okay
I'm trapped

CHAPTER 8
Pocketbook

Pam became friendly with the other women in the two-story, four-unit apartment building in Leimert Park. Like her, all of them were single mothers just trying to survive. But that wasn't the only thing they all had in common. They also liked to smoke weed and drink alcohol. Soon enough, Pam's house became "party central." There was Amanda and her fifteen-year-old daughter McKenna, who lived directly above Pam and Seanette. Then there was Faith and her six-month-old daughter Hope, who lived across from Amanda and McKenna. And there was Zaire and her ten-year-old son Rashad, who lived directly across from Pam and Seanette.

Rashad and Seanette had the common interests of drawing, playing board games and reading. He was also a natural artist and was wise beyond his years. He seemed so knowledgeable about the world. He was five years older than Seanette, so initially, she looked up to him as a big brother. She was drawn to him and he told her he would always look out for her.

Rashad didn't start off molesting Seanette. In fact, he was very protective. He played it smart. His angle was to build a trusting relationship with her first. They'd go to each other's houses to play board games, draw, play video games, or just hang out and read. He would read comics and sci-fi books while Seanette did crossword puzzles. They spent a lot of evenings in Rashad's room, unattended, with the door closed.

One evening, Rashad and Zaire came over to hang out. While their mothers were getting loaded in the living room, Rashad and Seanette were playing a board game in her room. As the game dragged on, Rashad grew bored. Seanette suggested they play another game. Every game that she suggested, Rashad didn't want to play. Rashad came up with the bright idea of making a clubhouse under the bed. Seanette was very gullible and agreed with Rashad, because he always had good ideas. She never had a hunch or a bad feeling. She trusted him. He was always nice to her.

Rashad got under the bed and told her to follow. Without any questions, she did just what he said. Once under the bed, he told her they had to hide from the adults. From underneath the bed, they could see the adults' feet whenever they opened the bedroom door. Seanette giggled. She liked to play hide-and-seek, something Rashad suggested they do whenever he got bored with any other games or activties.

At first, Rashad loved to hug and kiss Seanette passionately. He said it was okay, because he loved her. Gradually, he started touching and sucking on her undeveloped bare chest, and also made her grope his erect penis. After the "game" would be over, he would always get really agitated and hostile towards her. There was never a discussion or explanation about these incidents. He just acted as if they never occurred. Soon, he distanced himself from Seanette, telling her she was too young to play with anymore.

One day, when Seanette came home from school, she noticed a lot of cardboard boxes packed and lined up in front of Zaire's door. They were moving! No one knew the reason or where they were headed. Rashad never said goodbye, and Seanette never saw him again.

After Zaire moved away, Pam started hanging out more with Amanda from upstairs. She often sent Seanette up there to hang out with McKenna while she got high. Pam usually put Seanette off on other people for that reason.

By this time, Seanette was six years old. She liked going upstairs to hang out with McKenna. She looked up to the fifteen year old because McKenna seemed interested in Seanette's hobbies and treated her like a little sister. She paid attention to Seanette and always wanted to play with her, which made Seanette feel important.

Seanette enjoyed playing with McKenna's fashion doll "Paris" and the entire collection of accessories for this highly popular toy at the time—the cars, houses, clothes, boats and swimming pool. Pam thought Seanette was too young to own the fully developed Paris doll, insisting she wait until she was thirteen before having one, so McKenna said it could be their little secret.

McKenna combed Seanette's hair, too. She would compliment her on how "good" her long, jet-black hair was. She always brushed it in the latest styles, which Pam would never approve of. Pam did not permit Seanette to wear her hair down or in her face. "Only fast girls wear bangs or their hair down," she would say. McKenna was meticulous and thorough to always put Seanette's hair back exactly the way Pam styled it, as she did not let anyone but family comb or play in it.

One day, while Seanette was visiting, McKenna pulled out a stack of magazines and invited Seanette to look at them with her. McKenna moved from the floor to the top bunk of her bed with the magazines and asked Seanette to climb up with her. Without hesitation, Seanette obliged, excited because she thought the magazines had paper doll cut-outs.

When Seanette reached the top mattress, she saw that McKenna was lying down naked, touching her "pocketbook." That was Diane's name for vagina. Seanette was confused; it was her first time seeing a naked female body or even a magazine filled with pictures of naked women.

McKenna sexually abused Seanette for the next two years. She'd coerce Seanette by always combing her hair first and telling her how pretty she was. The physical interaction would progress from there, including McKenna instructing her on how to perform oral sex. She would flatter Seanette often and even gave her special pet names. She never forced herself on Seanette. She was always gentle from beginning to end during every incident, and she always maintained eye contact. McKenna was beautiful to young Seanette, who did not realize the touching was wrong. No one had ever told her. Really, as a grade-school-aged child, Seanette felt indebted to McKenna. After all, McKenna always combed Seanette's hair in the prettiest styles.

Rashad and McKenna were the first to molest Seanette, but they were not the last. There were several others. Seanette never told a soul. Before long, just like Rashad, McKenna and her mother Amanda also moved away. But the damage to Seanette's mind, body and soul was already done. But the worst was yet to come.

Daddy's Chocolate Girl

I hear you call my name like a faint whisper in the wind
You serenade me with the familiar composition
From beginning to end
Yes, I am
delighted on how
you arranged it notably for me
I hope you lend me more of your time.
I yearn to know your fears and dreams
Your thoughts on what life really means

CHAPTER 9

Picture Perfect

Seanette felt the sun shine across her face as she raced Dominic across the playground onto the swing. "Wee! Wee!" she exclaimed. "Up! Up! And away!" She and Dominic could hardly wait to get on the swing. They had an ongoing contest every recess to see who could swing the fastest and highest. With exuberant giggles, she swung higher and higher and the wind blew her long, twisted ponytails. The swings were always a place of solace for Seanette.

Occasionally, Seanette would spot Sean standing outside the playground gate. His beck-and-call was very distinctive. He would call her name once, followed by a series of various whistled pitches, like a flute. The sound would immediately capture Seanette's attention because it was so beautiful to her. She was happy to see him, and he always managed to show up at just the right time. Even though he was unpredictable, she didn't care. He was entertaining to watch in action. He was a popular and gregarious man who made her laugh. With Sean, everything was impulsive, flashy and excessive—his big, fancy cars, house, wardrobe and, most of all, his promises to his daughter.

On this occasion, Seanette couldn't scamper to the fence fast enough, panting and gasping for air from running. As she approached her father, enthusiasm and anxiousness flooded her being at the same time. Still, she was too curious not to go. With fervency in his voice, Sean whispered, "When school is over, come right out the gate. I have a surprise for you." Throwing caution to the wind, she vigorously nodded in agreement. He then sealed the conversation the way he always did, with his signature means of saying goodbye, "Kool-Aid."

Needless to say, countless fantasies flooded Seanette's mind. "Oh, boy!" she thought. "Maybe this is the day he'll tell me how much he loves me" and not just try to buy her love with another special present. She longed for him to literally get to know her, the real Seanette. She reminisced about the promises he made to her. He said he'd come back for her. He promised they'd live together, with a maid to take care of her, after he finished his business out of town. He promised to make a better life, a rich life for them. He promised it was only going to be for a little while longer. Maybe now the wishing was over. At last! This dream was going to be brought to full fruition!

These were the thoughts Seanette entertained for the rest of the day until, eventually, the school bell rang. That set her emotions into high gear. She briefly contemplated what she should do if her mother found out. However, in spite of the impending consequences, she opted to take her chances. After all, Sean did say he had a surprise. Seanette ran to her father and jumped in the front seat of his canary yellow Cadillac with the personalized plate, "Sir Sean." The year was 1980 and Seanette was seven years old.

Sean always let Seanette sit close to him in the front seat. This made her feel special. He would ride her through the city and divulge stories of his adventures. Seanette was very impressionable and was mesmerized by her father. He had an interesting perspective on life. He was so animated. Engaging people in conversation was a craft. He had a charismatic aura about him that was intoxicating. It was like watching the lead character recite a monologue in a Tony Award-winning Broadway play. As he talked, he declared to Seanette that his priority mission was to educate her on "street life." Then he laughed hysterically, "You got book knowledge from your momma, and street knowledge from me!" Seanette didn't quite understand what he meant, but she took plenty of mental notes, watching everything and everybody.

Sean was remarkably discerning about Seanette's perception and intuition. He prided himself on sharing his personal business endeavors with her. He trusted her. He knew anything he ever told her or did in front of her was a secret. Their secret. He warned her not to share anything with Pam, making it clear that if Pam knew about "their business," she would terminate all contact.

Seanette felt honored that her father was so candid around her. In her mind, they were best friends. She only wished her mother would be so forthcoming around her.

Sean glamorized and glorified his lifestyle. Like Pam, Sean was known by two identities. To his business associates, he was Sean, while his street hustler handle to his "potnas" was "Bo."

Sean confided to Seanette that he was a pimp. In fact, as bizarre as it was, he was proud to actually show her his photo album of prostitutes. He kept this collection of Polaroid pictures—his "Gentlemen's Book of Ladies"—on his person at all times. The women were of different races and were dressed and posed provocatively. Sean had a strange, haughty, boisterous tone while flipping through this "catalog," made for the convenience of potential "johns." Seanette asked why he had the women posing that way. He replied, in a perfect British accent, "So the gentlemen can see what the ladies look like and to make sure they get what they pay for."

Sean reassured Seanette the ladies were safe and that he was effective at keeping them employed. He insisted he was a "good" pimp, who kept them dressed in the latest fashion. Still, he did emphasize that they knew, like everybody else, that Bo didn't play 'bout his "snaps," a term he used for money.

Sex trafficking was not Sean's only "occupation." He was also a drug dealer as well as a user, which is why he was always in and out of town, to make frequent drops and deals. He also did fraudulent automobile accidents like Pam.

Seanette's first stop with her father was always the liquor store. She followed him to the beer section and watched intently as he reached for two tall cans. Beer and cigarettes were his staples.

Sean told Seanette to get whatever she wanted while he put the beer on the counter. This was what Seanette loved about going to the liquor store with her dad, because she could always get the one thing she could never get with Pam: unlimited junk food.

Eating food gave Seanette a sense of control, power and security. Food always seemed to be a comfort for her. It never hurt her feelings. It was always around and available. Through both good times and bad, and everything in between, food pledged stability, affection and attention to Seanette. It was her closest companion. Seanette tossed all the junk food imaginable on the counter. "Why not use him to get her needs met?" she figured.

Sean then exchanged small talk with the store clerk, asking if he remembered his daughter. He seemed to express that phrase, "my daughter," out of his mouth automatically to everyone they met. He seemed to be parading her around town as if she had just come home from boarding school, when she and Pam lived no more than five miles from him.

Sean continued bragging to the clerk about what a great lawyer his daughter was going to be. Seanette was pleasantly accustomed to this regular routine. Sean recited his signature phrase, "That's my girl," that would have her on cloud nine. He made her feel so special. Seanette had no intentions of practicing law, but she went along with his dream as she enjoyed the attention he gave her. Sean told everyone how intelligent she was and how she got straight A's in school. Seanette learned at an early age the secret to keeping her parents happy. It was simple: be an overachiever. She felt invincible, like she was the smartest person on the planet—well, at least in her father's eyes. That's all that mattered.

As the sun began to set, Sean drove to his apartment. Though they only stayed a few minutes, it left a lasting impression on Seanette. Sean lived in a duplex apartment on Arlington Street on the westside of Los Angeles. He told Seanette the duplex was a condominium he was renting temporarily while his mansion was being built. He had a huge living room with a black playpen furniture set. There was a huge glass table in the middle of the room and a gigantic fish tank with assorted fish in the corner against the wall. The kitchen was the smallest room in the house. His bedroom was average-sized and had a waterbed with red silk sheets. The décor throughout the apartment all matched.

Sean's bedroom had a small walk-in closet with several shoeboxes stacked inside. He informed Seanette that the boxes contained money he was saving for her college education. He told her he was working hard so that he could retire at age thirty and spend more time with her. That's the explanation he gave for missing her birthdays, holidays (including Christmas), school breaks, and all school functions. Further, he claimed to have a trust fund and reassured her that she would never have to want for anything. Seanette never actually saw what was inside any of those shoeboxes, nor did Sean ever show her any documentation regarding a trust.

Finally, they left his house and headed to THE SURPRISE! But as Sean pulled into Toys "A" LOT, Seanette was devastated. Even though he told her she could get whatever she wanted, it was just not what she really wanted. She wasn't being ungrateful; she just didn't want another toy, more clothes, not even food at this point. She just wanted her parents' time. TIME! TIME! All she ever wanted was their TIME.

Seanette put on a façade and scanned the shelves up and down the aisles. She was in search of something that Toys "A" LOT most certainly could not give her, and she was completely frustrated. She randomly picked up toys and threw them in the cart. She picked up all sorts of "Paris" merchandise: dolls, cars, clothes and houses. She even picked toys she didn't particularity like. She was so hurt, and she wanted her father to hurt just the same. If she couldn't inflict pain in his heart, she would inflict it through his wallet. Meanwhile, Sean was laughing and smiling ear to ear the entire time, thinking they were having a wonderful time. NOT! He was so oblivious. He never understood Seanette only wanted his time.

Sean then drove Seanette home. As they slowly approached Pam's place, Seanette could see the police lights' shadow on the apartment building, trees and sky. She knew this was not going to be good. Pam was hysterical. Sean got out of the car and the two of them began screaming and cussing. He tried to explain to the police that it was his designated day for visitation. He opened the trunk of his car revealing to the police all of the toys. The police looked at Pam and she was fuming. As for Sean, he left that night with the toys still in his trunk.

Sean was good at manipulating situations in his favor, even if it meant using his own daughter to do it. He knew his shenanigans that day would set Pam off and make her look like the bad guy.

Meanwhile, Pam commanded Seanette to go inside. Seanette was so scared and started to cry as she walked in. But then, she remembered the bag of candy she had gotten at the liquor store. She was relieved. She was not totally alone. She had her constant companion: food.

Seanette went to her room to stash the candy in her underwear drawer. But before she could—cold busted! She didn't expect her mother to follow her. Pam immediately grabbed the bag of candy and threw it in the trash. Seanette was wounded but, like everything else, she just tucked it away deep in the pit of her soul.

Fantasy Land

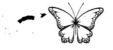

Deep inside
My very own magical place
I can roam free
Angels guide and protect me
Please keep my mind and soul at peace

CHAPTER 10

Happy Endings?

By now, Sean's visits with Seanette had grown fewer and farther between. This was partially due to his growing addictions and fast lifestyle, but also, Pam was now dating a man named Damon, and Sean did not like this at all. He was still very much in love with Pam and allowed himself to believe this other guy was stealing his family. He was determined to end their relationship at any cost, sparing no casualties.

Pam and Damon had become quite an item. Damon seemed like a breath of fresh air to Seanette. He presented himself as a well-rounded, responsible person. He had his own apartment and even attended evening classes at the local community college. Furthermore, he spent quality family time with both Pam and Seanette. They ate at the dinner table as a family every night, he helped Seanette with her homework in the evenings, and he took them both to the movies. He even took Seanette to class with him. Seanette liked Damon. He appeared to be genuinely caring, stable and consistent, and he was nice to her and her mother. Seanette had grown tired of watching her father hurt and disrespect her mother, so she was elated to see her mother happy. Frankly, she didn't want to see her momma cry ever again.

Damon had a daughter named Latricia, but everyone called her "Tricie" for short. He would drive out to Riverside every other weekend to pick her up. Tricie was the same age as Seanette and the two girls instantly bonded. They were like two peas in a pod. Soon, Damon moved in with Pam and Seanette, and Tricie also moved in permanently when her mother's drug habit spiraled out of control.

When Tricie arrived, she had severe head lice and a few tattered belongings, but Seanette didn't care. She was just so overjoyed to share her room. She loved having a sister—someone who authentically loved her, not for her toys or her body, but for her. Moreover, she had someone to talk to and play with. Not to mention, the molestation by McKenna stopped when they moved in, which greatly relieved Seanette. Pam drove Damon and Tricie out to Diane's and Otis' house and they, along with Regina, Desiree and Angel, embraced them all as family. Life was grand!

Unfortunately, not everyone was as accepting of this new and unconventional union. In particular, Seanette's parochial school. Pam enrolled Tricie into the same Christian school and when the teachers overheard the girls acknowledge one another as sisters, they questioned them about it since Tricie had a different last name. In an unmannerly way, the teachers advised the girls that they were not sisters. Then, the principal called Pam into the office and insisted she marry Damon, since they were already all living under one roof. The principal even threatened to expel Seanette unless they complied. So, Pam and Damon got married, and Damon became a father figure to Seanette. She felt comfortable with calling him "Daddy" because she saw him constantly.

The year was 1981 and Seanette was eight years old. The next two years would then pass by in a blur; there were so many transitions in the family's dynamics.

First, Seanette found out almost immediately that Damon lived a double life. His friends called him "Demon," and he was just that. It was Damon who introduced Pam to blue collar crime, which was through his involvement with the underground organization called "The Machine" that conducted fake car accidents, sold drugs and orchestrated other crimes. It was also Damon who introduced Pam to PCP, "sherm" and angel dust.

Around this time was when Pam hooked back up with her and Sean's old vocational school friend Debbie, as she found out through the grapevine that Debbie was now a drug dealer. Debbie sold PCP, heroin, pills, weed and cocaine, and soon, she was Pam's and Damon's main supplier. By now, Debbie had two children, Tykwana, or "Wana," who was two years younger than Seanette; and Tyrone, "Ty" for short, who was five years younger. Generally, Seanette accompanied Pam and Damon on these drug runs to Debbie's house and was sent to the room to play with Wana and Ty while Pam and Damon got high and purchased more drugs.

Damon persuaded Pam to start selling, making and using PCP in their home, where he was already growing and selling marijuana. He was very careless. He was not discreet about his drug business or use at all. Seanette found assorted paraphernalia all around the house, such as small brown bottles with sherm residue, used plastic resealable baggies with a white, powdery substance, a scale for weighing drugs, loose marijuana and rolled joints, and a huge potted weed plant in the kitchen. Damon also dealt drugs in clear view of Seanette.

Seanette didn't like this at all. She knew it was common for Pam to throw parties, smoke weed and drink with her friends, but Damon had an entirely different makeup of friends. They were sleazy. These people were bonafide drug addicts, hangers-on and losers. And they were jealous of Pam, rapidly dragging her down with them. The house was always filled with these low-lifers; there was constant traffic with strange people coming and going because it was the meet-up spot for Damon's friends to buy and smoke drugs. These people were loud and obnoxious as they constantly plotted the next come-up scheme. They had no respect for the home, staying all hours of the night, even on school nights. That family time, homework help and dinners at the table together Seanette used to enjoy with her mother and Damon came to an abrupt halt. She and Tricie were now ordered to complete their own homework and eat dinner most nights in their room.

The girls were instructed to only come out of their room to use the bathroom. Seanette was very curious, though. She noticed the rapidly evolving changes and needed to know what it was all about. So, she made all kinds of excuses to venture out. She asked for water. She faked an illness. She pretended to be afraid. She wanted her mother to say her prayers with her. She offered to take her mother's plate into the kitchen. She begged to be tucked in at night. She requested a bedtime story. On and on the pleas would come until, before long, Pam refused to oblige her. And soon thereafter, Pam started exhibiting uncontrolled anger towards her. From there, these angry outbursts turned into physical abuse.

One morning, Seanette woke up bright and early. It was third grade school pictures day, and she was so excited. She quickly got dressed, ate a bowl of cereal and brushed her teeth. Self-sufficiency at this stage was common for her. She accepted the role, as it was part of the new rules set in place when Damon moved in. She had no other choice but to take care of herself. Besides, it was also not out of the ordinary for Pam to sleep late, which always happened after a night of partying. Seanette knocked on her mother's bedroom door and eagerly waited for a response. When Pam opened the door, Seanette could tell she was already highly agitated.

Pam told Seanette to find hair ribbons and to put her school sweater on, but Seanette didn't know where either of them were. She searched the dresser for the hair ribbons and checked the drawers and the closet for the sweater, with no luck. That's when Pam started to yell and scream, demanding that she find that sweater, or else.

Pam grabbed Seanette by the arm and pulled her into the room. Stomping, cussing and threatening her daughter, Pam started pulling clothes out of the dresser onto the floor. She then dragged her by the arm to her closet and violently rummaged through the hung-up clothes. Behold, the sweater was there all along. Seanette had carelessly overlooked it. Pam then snatched the sweater off the wire hanger hard enough for the hanger to fly off the rack and onto the floor. She picked up the hanger and proceeded to beat Seanette with it—on her arms, her legs, her back and her face. Cowering on the closet floor, sobbing uncontrollably, Seanette begged her momma to stop. But Pam was too enraged. She continued to strike her over and over again with the hanger. At one point, Seanette let out a piercing squeal. The wire hanger had struck her eye. That's when Pam finally stopped. Needless to say, Seanette had to take her school picture that day with a swollen eye. Her mother never apologized; she just attributed the injury to a natural consequence.

Seanette struggled with whether or not she should tell anyone about that awful beating. After all, she had kept so many secrets from everyone, what difference would it make? By this time, she was a total co-dependent. She always put the feelings and wishes of both her parents before her own. And now, she had become terrified of her mother.

Periodically, Seanette still visited Auntie Regina and her daughters Desiree and Angel. By now, Desi was in college but came home over the breaks, so these visits were mostly over summer, and Diane and Auntie Regina would take the three girls to all the local amusement parks—Magic Mountain, Disneyland and Knott's Berry Farm. Seanette had a lot of fun with Angel and Desi. She felt safe and normal when she was with them. She trusted them.

It was during one of those visits that Seanette told Desi about the violent beating Pam gave her on school picture day. Shortly thereafter, while Seanette was at school, Desi rode the city bus there and told the principal what Seanette had said. The principal summoned Seanette out of class and interviewed her. Seanette told the principal and his wife (the assistant principal) what happened. Well, they called Pam. She was incensed. She came to the school absolutely outraged and flat out denied the accusations in front of everyone. She coerced Seanette to recant her story in front of Desi, the principal and his wife, and Seanette obeyed. She also lost all hope that day. She knew she was on her own, that no one was going to save her. She. Was. Alone. Seanette mentally buried yet another traumatic event deep into her soul.

It would be years before anyone from the family ever intervened on her behalf. Until then, Seanette was convinced this was how her life would always be. As a result, she shut off all of her emotions. She became numb and aggressively pursued comfort and affection from food and her predators. These were the only consistent, predictable, reliable fixtures in her life.

Somewhere in all this hurt and confusion, Sean reappeared into Seanette's life. Like always, he continued to use "going out of town on business" as the excuse for missing her important events. What also never changed was showing up with the most outrageous gifts as overcompensation for lost time. On one occasion, he even showed up on the doorstep with a live rabbit—no cage, no food, just a white rabbit. Of course, Seanette wanted to keep it, but her mother was utterly dumbfounded and made Sean leave and take it with him. Needless to say, Sean was mad.

After being missing in action for several months, Sean came to the house unexpectedly one evening to visit with Seanette. He banged on the door and demanded access to his daughter. Pam strictly adhered to the court orders but also knew that if she gave him an inch, he'd take a mile. She refused to let him in but reminded him through the door about the visitation schedule. Sean became so infuriated that he put his fist through the glass panes on the side of the door. Damon feared Sean (Sean bullied him with pride), so he just opened the door and offered Sean some of the spaghetti Pam had just made for dinner.

Pam's days of being afraid or even intimidated by Sean were long gone. And it didn't hurt that, unbeknownst to Sean, she had purchased a .38 Special revolver and taken lessons. So, while Damon stuttered and struggled to keep Sean calm, Pam got the gun and pointed it directly at Sean. That was the last domestic violence incident Seanette ever witnessed between her parents.

But revenge was a code Sean lived by, breathed and fed off of. He never forgot the day Pam pulled a gun on him.

Time Stood Still

Total silence
A complete blur
Where is my momma?
Why can't I find her?
Everything is moving fast
Wishing
Praying
The last 30 seconds of my life could forever . . . last
No hope
Total despair
I am alone
I am afraid
I am abandoned

CHAPTER 11

Total Chaos

The drug traffic grew noticeably heavy inside the home. Damon and Pam were in full throttle, selling and using drugs both inside and outside the apartment. They seemed to have tunnel vision about the world and their responsibilities. Seanette felt that nothing else mattered or existed to them and that she was an insignificant burden. She hated this "new normal." It made her withdraw and distance herself from the present reality into her fantasyland, and she constantly daydreamed of a better life. She was under the assumption that her "real" parents had been kidnapped and were being held captive in a locked closet somewhere. This was her truth. Soon, she imagined, she would be rescued away from Pam, Sean and Damon.

Why did they use drugs? And why did they hang around such low-life people? Seanette was ashamed of her parents' reckless and selfish lifestyle, and she hated drugs. Drugs ruined her life. They were the defining, unrelenting source of all the incessant chaos, peril and despondency in her life. Drugs replaced a child's devotion with hate. Seanette hated Damon for taking her mother away, she hated Pam for not protecting her, and she hated Sean for always lying to her. She hated them all.

Even more so, she hated herself. Seanette hated herself for not having the courage to speak up. She desperately wanted the confidence to tell them the colossal effects their actions directly had on her life. The molestation. The extraordinary incompetence she felt every day about her school work (especially math). Her plummeting low self-esteem and the overwhelming depression. Her constant state of fear and anxiety that caused infrequent bowel movements. Her newly stout shape due to a worsening, unhealthy dependency on food. Seanette felt ugly and disgusting. She felt her hair was cursed. It signified anguish. It was a constant reminder of the consequences of being vulnerable and naïve. Seanette hated everything about herself. She felt stupid and incompetent and just wanted to die. No wonder she fantasized all the time, creating in herself a daily anticipation for her "real parents"—whoever they were—to find her and retrieve her out of this toxic environment.

In the meantime, she daydreamed about her friends, the butterflies. She imagined herself in an open field, somewhere alone and safe. She envisioned herself flying high in the sky with wings of purple hues, surrounded by various colors and species of butterflies. With the blue skies offering serenity and a gentle breeze providing a soothing caress, her fears subsided. She felt strong. She felt confident. She felt secure. She felt fearless. Whenever Seanette felt scared, in danger or confused, this daydream would be her refuge. It gave her hope. She promised herself she would get out of that environment one day, and she trusted God for it. She would have her own nice and normal family, with a devoted husband who loved God, and wonderful children. She would be successful and live out all her dreams. Yes, she had to get out, and never look back. That's what she vowed to herself.

It was a school night. There were no signs and no warning. Nothing out of the ordinary had occurred that day. Damon's daughter Tricie and Seanette were watching television in their room. All of a sudden, a bunch of men burst in. They were all wearing black jackets with "DEA" in white letters on the back. A police raid! Seanette was quickly ushered upstairs to Faith's apartment. Her momma was gone. Damon was gone. She never saw Tricie again.

Seanette cried on Faith's living room floor. Faith attempted to console her, but she just didn't know what to say. Seanette wanted to go home, but Faith said she couldn't. When Seanette asked for Pam, all Faith could say was, "Everything will be okay." Seanette sucked her thumb and held on to her favorite stuffed animal, "Stuffie." It was a white lamb that played music. Diane had given it to her. She fell asleep and later woke up to Diane's voice. Otis carried her downstairs to the car. They had grabbed a few of her belongings and then headed back to the San Fernando Valley. The drive seemed like an eternity. It was very cold. Seanette was shivering. The sky was pitch black.

Finally, they arrived at the house. Diane made Seanette some hot chocolate and gave her some iced oatmeal cookies. She knew they were her favorite. That's when she asked Seanette did she want to live with them or still live with her mother. Seanette asked where her mother was. Otis told her that Pam was in jail and they didn't know when she was getting out. Diane then added, "We are going to put up our house for her to get out. I hope she doesn't run off."

Seanette felt a surge of guilt and undue responsibility. "I wish they weren't leaving the decision all up to me," she thought. "Sure, I hate Momma, but that's because of the drugs. The drugs are the problem, not Momma." Then she thought, "Maybe now that this happened, things will be different. Surely, they have to be different." So, with that, she stopped mentally deliberating with herself and quickly said, "I want to go home with my mother." "Okay, we will get her out," Diane replied. So, Diane and Otis put their house up for Pam to be released from jail.

Seanette had to wait to see her mother for what seemed like an eternity. First, before they had Pam released from jail, Diane and Otis, along with Otis, Jr. (who was now back at home) moved all of her and Seanette's belongings from the apartment to storage. Seanette had only a handful of things because much was stolen in transition. Even the beautiful convertible Cadillac was gone. Even harder, Seanette never got to say goodbye to Stacy, Tom the mailman, her friends at school, not even her father. She felt like she was in the Twilight Zone. One day she's at school and then overnight, her entire life has changed. And there was nothing she could do about it. She had no closure, and no one talked about what happened. She was totally confused and shattered. She was counting on her mother to have some answers for her.

When Pam returned, Seanette was overjoyed to see her and flew into her arms. Seanette learned from her mother that it was Sean who tipped the police off, and also that he was the first person to visit her in jail. But that was it. Her mother never said anything further about what happened, not an explanation or even an apology. So, Seanette once again locked away yet another traumatic event deep into her soul.

Seanette assumed, now that her mother was out of jail, they could return to their apartment in Leimert Park. That was Seanette's home. But no one bothered to tell her that going back home was simply not an option. In fact, everyone just acted like the entire incident never happened. So, she and her mother ended up living at Diane and Otis' house. Initially, Seanette enjoyed being at their house. She could spend more time with her cousin Angel. But after playing outside, watching television and eating dinner, Angel went home with Auntie Regina until the next Sunday family dinner. Once again, Seanette was all alone.

After Pam got out of jail, she was rarely at home. She didn't cook for Seanette or help with her homework. She just wasn't there. Seanette wasn't sure where her mother went whenever she left, but she was always in such a hurry. Seanette was determined to find out why.

Seanette felt completely out of place at her new school. She went from attending a predominately African-American Christian school to attending a public school with a large Hispanic population. It was culture shock. At her old school, everyone had brown faces, from the principal to the teachers, staff and all the students. Here, she had no friends and no rapport with her teachers. At her old school, everyone was close-knit. The teachers even remembered and celebrated the children's birthdays.

Seanette had to walk to and from school by herself because her mother wouldn't drive her. This was puzzling to her because Pam drove her every day at her previous school. Still, Seanette made the best out of the situation. She took an interest in a couple of school plays and got both parts she tried out for. One was a holiday play, and the other was a poetry reading. Diane was instrumental for the play, helping Seanette with her costume, and even combing her hair and spraying it with temporary gray hair dye. To Seanette's delight, her mother also got involved by helping her memorize her lines.

The day of the play, Seanette was so excited. It was an evening performance and she went over the date and time with everyone so they wouldn't be late. Diane took off of work to make sure she was there on time, and Otis was already at home. But Pam was nowhere to be found. Seanette waited and waited for her mother and was nearly late to rehearsal, so Diane insisted they leave without Pam. During the play, Seanette frequently scanned the crowd to see if her mother had arrived. Seanette was onstage, mid-sentence of her monologue when she noticed Pam slip through and stand by a side door. The room was crowded, and all the seats were taken. Seanette froze on stage. She recognized the blank expression on her mother's face, that grave sign that she was high. Pam was smoking Sherm again.

They stayed with Diane and Otis for about six months to a year. Seanette still didn't know anyone, and she barely saw her mother. Pam always came home late at night, well after Seanette's homework and dinner were done and she was in bed. Seanette would look out the bedroom window and wait for Pam to come back, but she would grow tired and fall asleep. She and her mother shared a room, so when Pam did come back, Seanette felt her cold body get in the bed. Diane got tired of Pam coming home late. She gave her a ten o'clock curfew so that, if she wasn't in the house by then, she was locked out for the night. This happened a lot.

Pam had reconnected with her old high school buddies Patricia, Clara and Linda. Her addiction became more real to Seanette while they were staying with Diane and Otis, because Pam started taking her along on her ventures. Not by Pam's choice, either. She and Diane argued constantly about her being gone all the time and not spending any quality time with Seanette. Seanette, on the other hand, was glad, partly because she wanted to know where her mother went all the time. She knew Pam was getting high, but also, she assumed her momma was preparing for them to move into their own place. She thought things were going to turn around.

Boy! Was she in for a big surprise! Pam did not spend time with Seanette alone at all. She and Seanette only went to three or four places total whenever they left Diane and Otis's house: the liquor store, the projects so she could buy Sherm, a nearby park or a friend's house. Pam always went to the liquor store and bought malt liquor. Then, she would go to the Bottoms housing development to buy some Sherm, leaving Seanette to wait in the car. If she wanted to smoke it right away, she stood outside the car and smoked it. If she decided to wait, they went to the park.

Initially, Seanette was happy to go to the park. She thought Pam would push her on the swing, but this was not the case. First, as the two of them sat in the car, Pam put in a cassette tape. She usually played songs by The Temptations, like "Psychedelic Shack," "Cloud Nine" and "Runaway Child, Running Wild." Then she would play The Jackson Five—"The Love You Save," "Never Can Say Goodbye," "I Wanna Be Where You Are," "Mama's Pearl" and "Love Jones"—on repeat. Seanette always wondered what her momma was thinking about as she sat there.

While the songs played, Seanette would sit there and daydream about flying with the butterflies. And then her mother would open that malt liquor. Seanette would feel a knot forming in the pit of her stomach. Once her beer was gone, Pam would tell Seanette to go play in the park. But Seanette wasn't fooled. She knew the only reason they went to the park was so that her mother could smoke that Sherm. As soon as she got back in the car, the distinct stench lingered. It was a miracle they would make it home safely, without ever getting into an accident. Truly, God and His angels were watching over them. Meanwhile, Seanette's hatred for her mother grew like a cancer.

Play Cousins

Awakened from sleep
As you snag and rip my underwear down
I'm used to this routine – no emotion on the outside
Inside I wear a frown
My play cousin has many faces
They all have similar backgrounds
But live in different places
All but a handful are attracted to my pocketbook
No one told me to guard it or be concerned
If others wanted to take a look
The touching was sometimes subtle
Kind of like browsing in a clothing store
Other times it was forceful
Like an unlawful entry through a door
As you explore my motionless body
You stick your tongue in my mouth
Without even asking for my consent
Like an animal you violate me
You violently push my legs up until they're bent
It hurts
I remain silent
I don't understand
I feel you rubbing my bare undeveloped chest with your hand
Sticking objects in my pocketbook
From fingers to candy to even a hair brush
I'm squirming now
I'm afraid
I try to scream
I feel your hot breath on my ear

You whisper, "Hush"
I can't think
I feel helpless
As you continue to use me
As a volunteer for your
Twisted
Sick
Personal
Self-satisfaction
Are you thinking by now why didn't I take some kind of action
In my mind, countless times I asked myself
"What should I do?"
The room is spinning
My mind is only filled with thoughts of her
I must not disobey but listen too.
After all, each time
I tried in my own way to communicate
Your posture changed
You look at me with hate
In a very uncompassionate tone
You speak with utter doom
The phrase still echoes in my spirit
GO BACK INTO THE ROOM!!!

CHAPTER 12

Twisted Love

Before long, Pam met up with her old boyfriend from high school. Earl had a city job, but he was a chronic alcoholic, always drunk and with a half-pint of liquor of liquor in the back pocket of his jeans. Earl was always giving Pam money and even gave her a car, an old brown Plymouth. Pam told Seanette she was just using Earl, that he just worked out for "right now." She'd often brag about how, after getting him drunk, she would take all his money and give some to Seanette for school. Seanette hated taking that money. She felt sorry for Earl. He was nice and she didn't think it was right the way her mother took advantage of him.

While Pam was spending more and more time with her girlfriends, Seanette got lost in the shuffle. She couldn't relate to their children, and she hated the environment. But Pam made her refer to these women as her "aunties and godmothers." Pam and Seanette spent a lot of time at Pat's and Linda's houses because they lived close to Diane in the San Fernando Valley, while Kaneatra and Debbie still lived in Los Angeles. They could go down there only if they had gas money. Seanette viewed her mother as selfish and shifted the blame from Damon to her. It was clear to her that her mother was having the time of her life, while she felt helpless and alone. With these feelings nagging at her spirit every day, Seanette walked around dazed and confused all the time.

Seanette liked going over to Pat's house, though, because she always had food. Pat would let her eat until she was stuffed. Meanwhile, Pam would be outside smoking Sherm in Pat's parking lot. As she breathlessly gorged down the food, Seanette would watch her mother anxiously from the kitchen window, amazed at how quickly her mother would go from an alert and lively person to a ghastly, lifeless soul, in a matter of seconds.

Pat had three kids: Vanessa, Shay and Brent. Brent was eight years old, the same age as Seanette, but she rarely saw him because he was heavily involved in sports. At fifteen, Vanessa was the oldest and was beautiful to Seanette. She was light-skinned and Seanette viewed light-skinned people as being more acceptable. Seanette had developed a self-hatred and a deep-rooted inferiority complex about herself. Her physical attributes that she once considered her pride and joy — her thick, curly, jet black hair and her dark complexion — she now saw as grotesque because she had gained weight and had an awkward physique.

Vanessa had all the latest clothes, jewelry and hairstyles, and was very popular. She was also very voluptuous and every guy at her high school wanted her. She shared a room with her younger sister Shay, who was thirteen years old. Shay and Seanette had a lot in common, like the same texture of hair, and Shay was chubby, too. She was still very much innocent in some regards; for instance, she liked to play games, and they both played with stuffed dolls.

Seanette and Shay also enjoyed listening to music. Shay and Vanessa had all the latest records from teenage artists like New Edition, The Jets, Lisa Lisa and Cult Jam, Prince and, of course, Michael Jackson. Vanessa would play the records over and over until they knew all the words to the songs, and Shay had a great voice. This became a favorite pastime for Seanette because it reminded her of the days she sang with her mother. Seanette trusted Shay; she believed she had a friend, a true friend. Finally, she felt normal.

Shay didn't molest Seanette until almost six months into their friendship. It happened one night when Pam had gotten so high on Sherm that she and Seanette had to stay over Pat's house. She lived only about half a mile away, but before they went there, Pam drove to the Bottoms housing project to buy some Sherm. When they arrived at Pat's house, she and the kids weren't home yet, so Pam told Seanette to wait on the back porch steps while she went to the parking lot to smoke her Sherm.

Pat's apartment unit was in clear view of the parking lot, and Pam was standing only about three feet from Seanette. Seanette watched as her mother turned away from her, lit the Sherm cigarette and put it to her mouth. Seanette felt the knot enlarging in her stomach. The melancholy suffocated her. She loathed this feeling of fear and powerlessness. She had to silence it, but she didn't have any food to quell it. She didn't know what time it was, she just watched as the sun set over the roof of Pat's apartment.

Eventually, Seanette heard Pat's and her kids' voices coming from the front door. Pat parked her car on the street in front of the apartment building this time, and the children came in with grocery bags. Seanette was more than willing to help them bring the bags in because she was starving. Pat started making pork chops and gravy, spinach and potatoes for dinner.

As she cooked, Pat told Seanette to sit at the table to finish her homework. Before long, she immediately noticed Seanette daydreaming. Seanette was thinking about the clouds, the wind, blue skies and butterflies as a way to escape her struggles with math. Pat called Vanessa and Shay in to help her with her times tables, making a game out of it. All three of them were so encouraging and cheered Seanette on as she recited a few by memory. After dinner, she helped the girls clean up the kitchen.

All this time, Pam was still out in the parking lot smoking her Sherm. When she finally came in, everyone just stared at her. To try to normalize the situation, Pat asked Pam if she was "cool." Pam struggled to speak and cleared her throat a few times before finally being able to utter, "Yeah." She then found her way into the living room and stayed motionless on the couch. The happy atmosphere turned awkward.

Pat told all three of the girls to go into her daughters' room. Vanessa later left to be with her boyfriend, leaving Shay and Seanette to play with some of Shay's dolls and watch television for a while. When

Seanette noticed it had gotten dark outside, she went to go check on her mother. Pam was still out of it, so Pat said they would be spending the night. When Seanette went back to the room, Shay had gotten out a few packs of hard candy. Seanette loved candy and goodies in general, but she positively loved hard candy. Shay offered her a couple and then suggested they lie down on the bed.

Seanette was all too familiar with this "bed" routine and immediately felt uneasy. She second-guessed her doubts, though, because Shay was offering candy. None of her previous abusers had offered her candy or food. So, against her better judgment, she got in the bed with all her clothes on as Shay turned off the lights. Seanette noticed how the television glowed in the dark room. "Don't be afraid," Shay whispered. Shay had a piece of the candy in her mouth and asked if Seanette wanted to taste it. Seanette assumed that she was going to give her one out of the pack. Instead, Shay tried to kiss her with an open mouth. Seanette pushed her back in disbelief. Shay then mocked her for not knowing how to french kiss. Forcibly this time, Shay then kissed her again, placing the candy in her mouth. "See, that was okay, right?" Shay whispered again. Seanette didn't respond at all. She just laid there stiff. Shay then told her to take off her pants.

Seanette became frozen in time. She retreated to her made-up world with the butterflies. She tuned Shay out as Shay completely undressed her, teased her about her under-developed, prepubescent body, spread her legs, inserted a piece of candy into her pocketbook, and told her how sweet and innocent she tasted. Although Seanette did wince and squirm during this assault, she couldn't even hear what Shay was saying. Even when Shay asked her if she "came," besides not knowing what that meant, all she saw was her lips moving. Then, when Shay tried to make Seanette eat the offending piece of candy, Seanette was able to pull away. This was the only time Shay violated her, but not only did Seanette never trust her again, she was absolutely crushed. And once again, she crammed the pain deep within the pit of her stomach.

Within that six-month period, Pam's old friend Linda came back on the scene. Initially, Linda persuaded her and Pat to try cocaine.

Linda enjoyed freebasing, which is smoking cooked cocaine out of a glass pipe. Pam and Pat freebased from time to time, but they preferred snorting lines because they viewed it as sophisticated. Pam really enjoyed cocaine. It took her from being a motionless zombie to being hyper and erratic. Soon, Pam and Linda were serious running buddies.

Pam frequently drove to all of Linda's friends' houses to get high and, of course, she took Seanette with her. Seanette was falling further and further behind in school, which wasn't helped by the fact that her mother took no interest in attending back-to-school nights or parent-teacher conferences. Her only involvement in Seanette's education was to threaten her with, "You know what to do at school."

The visits with Linda, like with Pat, always occurred after school, so Seanette usually didn't eat dinner or do her homework. Linda and Pam would often say they were "going to the store" and then be gone for hours. With this signature statement from her mother, Seanette and Linda's son Hakeem were left alone in the apartment. Hakeem was five years older than Seanette, who was still a few months from being nine years old. She always felt uncomfortable because he reminded her of Rashad, the first boy who molested her. She stayed in the living room and watched television, while Hakeem stayed in his room playing video games.

Hakeem didn't wait long at all to molest Seanette, and he was a bully about it. He used the living room television as a sort of ransom, along with verbal and physical intimidation, to get what he wanted. She felt helpless because it was his house. That all too familiar knot swelled in her stomach whenever she had to go over there. And she prayed her momma would return before he had a chance to touch her. But that never happened. Usually, she'd be asleep on the living floor by the time Pam and Linda finally got back.

Hakeem was very demanding, forceful and vulgar, with no modesty at all. He would often prance around naked in front of Seanette and put his genitals in her face. Seanette had never seen a boy naked, and this was gruesome to her. He made her rub his genitals and perform oral sex on him, all the time promising that once she did, he would leave her alone and give her back the remote control. Sometimes he did, other times he didn't. His behavior was so erratic and intimidating, including sometimes punching her in the arm and pushing her around the house.

Hakeem was equally abusive emotionally. He said horrible things to Seanette in the midst of instructing her on how to please him. He repeatedly called her flat chested and fat and always ended with these cruel words: "This will just have to do." Then he would put his clothes on and completely ignore her, like she wasn't even there.

Once, while Linda and Pam were "gone to the store," Hakeem's cousin came over. Hakeem demanded that Seanette perform oral sex on his cousin, but when his cousin declined, Hakeem called him "gay" and ridiculed him to the point where he felt he had to prove otherwise. Hakeem laughed and made fun of both of them the entire time.

Seanette hated herself. She felt so cheap, so stupid. She felt like a piece of trash. She felt as if she had a neon sign on her forehead that said, "Molest Me." Why was this happening to her? And why didn't anyone else notice? But why dwell on the why's and how's. She was convinced this was how her life would be forever. That day, she accepted that she was worthless.

Out of the blue, Pam stopped going over to Linda's house. Seanette was glad! She didn't know why, and she didn't care. Back at Diane's house, though, things began to escalate.

Down in the Pit

I'm swallowed by your addictions
They infiltrate and destroy
Like a flooding hurricane
You have not a care in the world
You are living in the fast lane
I watch from the shadows
As you cook, snort, smoke, and freebase cocaine
Trying to understand
What satisfaction have you gained?
I am intrigued by your loyalty
Your dedication and drive
I overstuff myself with food
I want to run and hide
I am numb
I want to die
I am invisible
I am neither seen nor heard
I am not a priority
You couldn't care less
Simply not concerned
These were the lessons
The beliefs
From addiction
That I learned

CHAPTER 13
Smiling Faces

Diane initiated arguments with Pam more and more each day. They bickered all the time. The more they quarreled, the more Seanette hated living there. Most often, the bickering was about her. Diane criticized Pam about the way she dressed Seanette. She nitpicked about the way Pam combed Seanette's hair. According to Diane, everything Pam did was always done the wrong way.

The final straw for Pam came on Seanette's ninth birthday. Pam bought her a black-and-white mini dress with white leg warmers and white tennis shoes to match. Seanette was so happy because that was the only thing she asked for. "She looks like a prostitute in that dress," Diane said to Pam in front of Seanette. That made Seanette start to cry, and at that, Pam informed Diane they were moving out. They were leaving for the night and would be back for their things sometime in the week. Needless to say, Seanette's birthday was a total disaster. She and her mother ended up spending the night at Pam's friend Clara's house with her and her daughter Teresa.

Clara, or "CeCe," lived in a two-bedroom apartment in the Van Nuys area of the San Fernando Valley. Teresa shared her room with Seanette, and Pam slept in the living room on the playpen sofa. Teresa was four years older than Seanette. She was very nice to Seanette and never violated her. CeCe was a party girl who belonged to a motorcycle club, where she was known as "Candy." Pam and Seanette often accompanied her and other club members on outings. Pam seemed to be having the time of her life, but for Seanette, moving in with CeCe turned out to be a gigantic mistake. CeCe, like Linda and Pam, abused cocaine.

Pam quickly became a regular cocaine user. She still smoked PCP from time to time and drank a lot, but cocaine was becoming her favorite drug. As usual, Pam's swift shift in her behavior patterns turned Seanette into a private investigator. She had to know why Pam had so many mood swings. So, one night, Seanette snuck out of the bedroom in the middle of the night. When she opened the door, the music was blasting and the room was filled with assorted types of people. She watched as CeCe passed a flat glass mirror around with lines of cocaine on it. Everyone, including Pam, snorted the cocaine off the glass. They all seemed so jovial and carefree. Immediately, Seanette felt the knot in her stomach begin to swell and harden. "This is a different feeling," she thought to herself. But she shrugged it off, went back into the room and went to sleep.

Seanette hated living there. Her only outlets were swimming and junk food, and she escaped through both. CeCe had a pool in her apartment building and Seanette got up early on the weekends to swim for as long as she could. As for junk food, there was a drive-through dairy within walking distance where she buys all sorts of candy bars, cookies, chips and fruit pies. She would stuff herself until all her emotions were numb.

Pam knew her daughter didn't particularly like living with CeCe, but they had nowhere else to go. The move was only supposed to be temporary. CeCe's mother put Pam's name ahead on the list of a government housing agency she worked for that subsidized rent payments for low-income families. In the meantime, Pam found a private Christian school for Seanette to attend.

But first, the new school required that Seanette take a placement test. Unfortunately, she scored low for reading comprehension and even worse on the math equations. The school informed Pam that, in order for Seanette to be accepted, she would have to repeat the fourth grade instead of going into fifth grade for the upcoming school year. Predictably, Pam came down hard on Seanette for not scoring at least average on the assessment test, questioning what she had been doing all the previous years in school. Pam reprimanded her for not trying her best and for not telling her she needed help with her homework.

Pam decided to go ahead and enroll Seanette in the school, but she warned her not to fall behind for not applying herself. The school was about a thirty-five-mile car ride and a three-hour bus ride from CeCe's apartment. Pam still had the old brown Plymouth, but it started giving her problems all the time. The alternator, the engine, the brakes, the radiator—it was always something. So, Seanette had to take the bus to and from school alone, at nine years old.

Pam had been in touch with her close friend Joy, who told her Sean came by asking for Seanette. So, Pam promised to take Seanette to Joy's house for the weekend so she could spend time with him. Seanette couldn't wait to go! Joy and her husband Nathan truly had the love of Christ, and Seanette felt safe and happy at their house. She had peace of mind. She didn't have to worry about anything at Joy's house. No one tried to molest her there.

Joy's and Nathan's home was always filled with kids. Some were relatives and some, like Seanette, were adopted in. Regardless, they treated all the children as their nieces and nephews, and it never made a difference. Everyone had chores in the house, and when they were done, they were all rewarded. Nathan always bought doughnuts off the doughnut truck or ice cream off the ice cream truck that came through the neighborhood. Joy and Nathan took everyone to church, and after church, they'd take all the kids out to dinner at a local family-owned restaurant called Herb's. It was very affordable for families, and they always had specials. For a very low price, every kid could get a full meal, soup or salad, a drink and even a dessert. Seanette loved Herb's because she always had more than enough to eat.

Joy and Nathan were very serious about their relationship with Jesus. Joy loved Jesus. At home, she would openly praise God, belting out Gospel songs from her soul. "Through trials and tribulations, I made it over . . . He has been my mother and my father." Seanette always looked on in amazement as Joy would sing about Jesus. She could feel her sincerity. She knew Joy really meant it. She learned from Joy not only how to worship God, but why it was important. Joy praised God when she had food and when she didn't, and when she had money and when she didn't. She always had strong faith that God would provide, regardless of the circumstances. Besides that, Seanette loved just being around Joy. She was so maternal, so loving and understanding. Joy provided stability for Seanette. Her voice was so powerful and encouraging.

Although they lived on the east side of Los Angeles just a block away from the projects, everyone in the community respected Joy and Nathan. Joy's brothers and sisters had all moved away except her youngest sister Janet. She was all the kids' favorite aunt because she was the youngest, coolest and hippest "auntie." She and her newborn son shared a room with Joy's daughter Michele. Michele was about five years younger than Seanette, and the two of them became close. They always had fun together when they spent time over the weekends.

It was on a Friday evening when Pam pulled up to Joy's house. She told Seanette she would pick her up on Sunday after church. Seanette jumped out of the car and ran into Joy's house. Joy confirmed that Sean had been by a few times looking for her. Joy had told Sean she'd been in touch with Pam and that Seanette would be over that weekend. He promised to come by to pick her up, but he didn't leave his phone number. Seanette thought that was strange, being that the last time she saw him, he had a lot of money, a car and a condo he was renting.

Sean did pick Seanette up on Saturday, just as promised. He drove her to a park on Second Avenue. The two of them often went to this park, where he would play basketball with his friends while she ran up and down the grassy hills or played with other children. She always settled on the swings so she could get a front row seat to watch her father play, which she loved. Sean was very good and very competitive. He liked the physical contact. He was also quite good at social games like cards, dice and dominoes. He never lost, and he was merciless about it, wisecracking at his opponents and making sly, sarcastic remarks as he played and kept scoring. Sean was a winner, a very aggressive winner.

Usually after he won, Sean would come push Seanette on the swings until she couldn't handle it anymore. She'd laugh with glee and beg him to stop. This time, though, Sean didn't come to her but called for her from a far-off park bench. She quickly got off the swings and joined him. He uttered those familiar words, but this time with urgency: "I have a surprise for you, but you have to promise–" Seanette interrupted him before he could finish his sentence, "I promise! I promise!" Sean continued, "Well, I can't tell you right now, just promise." Seanette tried to reassure him, "I promise, I really do!"

She wondered to herself, "What could the surprise be? What could he want to tell me?" Then she wondered, could it be he was going to rescue her? Oh, boy! She could hardly wait! Or maybe it wasn't that big of a surprise, just more toys. The suspense was killing her.

But it was none of that this time. This time he really had a secret: Seanette had a sister.

A sister? Wow! Seanette's heart pounded with excitement. She couldn't believe it! A sister! This was better than anything imaginable that he could have given her. It was something that came from him and not a store. It wasn't money or food, no; this was a gift that took time. He used his time, and he wanted to share it with her.

Seanette wanted to see her sister, to hold her, to know her. Where is she? When could she see her? Sean and Seanette raced each other to the car, leaving the park she had come to cherish and that later she would learn was where her father slept on and off as his drug addiction grew worse.

Their first stop was, of course, the liquor store. This time, Sean purchased two "short dog" cans of malt liquor, half the size of the usual two tall cans, which he also bought. He put all four beers on the counter and told Seanette to get all the junk food she wanted. She picked up chips, chocolate, pastries and a soda. She and her dad then jumped back in the car and headed for the freeway. Seanette was beside herself, she kept asking if they would ever get there. Just as she was about to ask again for the umpteenth time, Sean pulled up to their destination.

Sean had already drunk a beer on the way there. When they got out of the car, before they went to the door, he handed Seanette a short dog. "Handle the beer." She struggled to open the can, so he did it for her and handed it back to her. Seanette took a sip. It was bitter and nasty. But Sean told her to keep drinking. She drank it all, and then her father gave her the second short dog can as they walked towards the house.

"Go ahead drink it." She was so eager to be a part of both of her parents' world that she hoped to herself, "Maybe this will make me happy like they are, experiencing the happiness they seem to have without any pain."

So, without a moment to waste, she gulped down the entire can as her father cheered her on. "Go on, girl, handle it. You got it, Baby Cakes." She couldn't believe all she had to do was drink with her dad to get his full attention. This seemed too easy.

When Seanette was finished with the second short dog, Sean told her to wipe her mouth with the back of her hand and get herself together. Once they entered the apartment, he introduced her to her sister Gia. Gia was six months old, and her mother Yolanda was sixteen years old. At the time, Sean was thirty-one and Seanette was nine. Yolanda also had another baby, a two- year old son by a different man.

Once Seanette laid eyes on her sister, there was an instant bond. She was so happy Pam allowed her to stay with him that weekend. She was looking forward to spending the entire time with her sister. Meanwhile, Sean kept disappearing and reappearing, making frequent trips back and forth to the store.

The night was young, and as Luther Vandross' Never Too Much album played, Sean, Yolanda and Seanette sang along and played dominoes. Sean also rolled a few marijuana joints. At first, he was just smoking with Yolanda. He then called Seanette over to him and gave her a "charge," taking a puff and then blowing the smoke directly into her mouth—all the while reassuring her that she could handle it.

Then, after a few more charges, he lit another joint and handed it straight to her. She took a hit once, and then her father instructed her to hit it again and again. Without a second thought, Seanette did what her father told her. Sean then got up and changed the music to The Whispers. While Chocolate Girl played, he danced around and sang to Seanette. "My father is the coolest person alive," she thought as she watched. She felt so much love and acceptance. She never felt like this before, it was inexplicable. Then she thought, "My mother never lets me come out of my room when she has company. Why did she want to hide it from me? Like my dad said, I can handle it."

Seanette felt so free. For one, she didn't have to worry about anyone trying to touch her or make her touch them. Beyond that, she wanted to tell her mother how she now knew and could relate to her world. Seanette wanted to get high with her. Maybe they could help each other and talk the way Seanette and her father did. But Seanette feared what would happen. Maybe her mother would take her away from Sean like he said. After all, he was her best friend and she believed everything he told her. He promised.

Sean, Seanette and Yolanda continued to smoke marijuana, drink beer and play dominoes. The higher Seanette got, the more they laughed at her. At first, they were all laughing together, but then they started making fun of her. Her new found sense of acceptance quickly turned into rejection. After a while, Sean and Yolanda disappeared into the bedroom to freebase cocaine and left Seanette alone in the living room with the two babies.

Seanette had never been around a baby or little children, so she had no clue what to do. When Gia began to cry, Seanette knocked on the door to tell them and Yolanda came out and handed Seanette a box of rice cereal. When Seanette asked for help, she told her to read the instructions. Seanette was so determined to show them she could handle the high. She never asked for help and made Gia the bottle. Yolanda returned from the room for a moment. Seanette thought she was going to help her with the little ones, but instead Yolanda threw a sheet on the couch and told her she could sleep there with Gia and Gia's brother.

The next day, it was as if nothing had transpired. Yolanda braided Seanette's hair into a cornrow style with beads all going toward one side of her face. When Seanette returned to Joy's house, her mother was waiting on the porch. Pam was furious when she saw Seanette's hair and yelled and screamed at her all the way back to CeCe's house. Pam made her take down all the braids, saying the style was too grown. All Seanette could think about was her sister. Breaking her promise to her father, she went ahead and told her mother about Gia, and Pam was livid. She told Seanette she didn't have a sister. Seanette felt the knot in her stomach stiffening.

Love?

Alone, I play with my friend the sun
You call me out of the light into the dark bedroom closet
I am not aware of the perversion from your soul to mine that
You intend to deposit
Oliver and Tina are there
How dare you compare
Whose turn it is next
Tina is scared
Oliver is a strong boy in physical stature
You're quite a match for her
You manipulated my mind
Tell me all acceptance and love I would find
If only I decide
I'm terrified and alone
I shed not one single tear
For fear you will see I am afraid
On my stomach you throw me like an old rag doll
I close my eyes hoping to see my imaginary friend the sunlight
There is no brightness in the entire room at all
My face is buried in an old worn mattress
I hear you gurgling as you accumulate a mouthful of spit
You aim it in between my buttocks
Like a dart hitting the bullseye
Making a direct hit
Conscious you are of your actions
My body has become your playground
Laughing in front of the crowd
Behind closed doors
You are a monster waiting to attack

No fight from me
I just keep looking back for help
But no one comes to my rescue
Above the blaring music
I hear my momma's voice
She yells for someone to pass her another brew
I wonder for a brief moment
Is this appropriate behavior
I smell the lingering aroma of different drugs
It's normal to me how the adults all savor
The all-night parties turn into sleepovers
Momma is too loaded to drive us home
Or is just plain passed out
I'm lying in a horror bed
I've given up and unable to shout
I'm no longer Momma's pride she loves to show off like a trophy
In my ruffled dress
I was her beautiful Indian princess
My once neatly twisted braids are a rat's nest
A total mess as the sun rises; the monsters become my friends
The terror from the night ends
With all my might
I fight to remain . . . sane

CHAPTER 14

Groundhog Day

A s Pam put the pedal to the metal on the 10 freeway, Seanette sang along with her to The Gap Band's song "Outstanding." Pam always had the radio tuned to station KJLH because it played all the jams. Seanette loved this song. It made her think of the apartment in Leimert Park, riding her Big Wheel, running through the flowers and trees, and playing with the butterflies. That's when she felt free. She rolled down the window, leaned her head out and closed her eyes as the wind hit her face. She loved how the sun kissed her skin. She always imagined it was God and His angels smiling on her.

Seanette just assumed her mother had more money since they were going to Los Angeles. The truth was, whenever they drove anywhere, they barely had gas. Today, the gas light seemed to glow brighter and brighter.

Soon, they were parked on the side of the freeway.

Pam put on the car's hazard lights and told Seanette to get out find a call box. Seanette didn't know what a call box was, which only caused her mother to yell at her. Seanette was afraid to get out of the car. It was scary seeing all the other cars speeding by. Pam got very frustrated and started cussing as she got out the car, slammed the door and opened the trunk to retrieve a gas can. She commanded Seanette to wait in the car while she went to get gas off the freeway. She then abruptly trekked down the emergency lane as Seanette watched and waited anxiously.

It was a long ride to Kaneatra's house. Seanette could feel the knot in her stomach tighten. The entire way there, she worried about seeing her predators, Kaneatra's kids. She was so sick of Tina and Oliver taking advantage of her body while their sister Audrey egged them on.

Then she thought how lucky her mother was, to escape and medicate the pain away. She was so jealous of her mother, but she also thought, was their abuse of her really her mother's fault? Seanette reverted to that usual, self-denigrating dialogue with herself. You did this. You caused this. You allowed them to have their way. You never said a word, so you deserve this. You are trash. So, this is the way it will always be. She wondered, how come her mother never asked her, "Why don't you like it in the room with the kids?" Fear, shame and rejection overwhelmed Seanette's entire being as the car traveled on.

More thoughts bombarded Seanette's mind. "Am I a bad girl?" In some respects, admittedly, she wanted those kids to touch and hold her, because she wanted love and attention. Or maybe she was just like them, fooling herself. And why not? After all, like it or not, she did have some things in common with them. Their parents got high together, and the kids weren't always mean to her. Sometimes they played the games that she liked, like jacks, cards, school or coloring. With all of this bombardment, Seanette's mind was in a permanent state of confusion. She decided the abuse was punishment for not being good enough, so she allowed herself to believe and expect that she deserved the worst out of life.

By now, Seanette was in a trance, but before she could punish herself with the thoughts any longer, Pam pulled up to Kaneatra's house. Seanette was hesitant to get out of the car, but Pam told her to get out. Kaneatra's house was red with a wide porch. The grass was brown and spotted. They had a ferocious dog they kept locked up under the house. Kaneatra's front door did not have a doorknob. The once eggshell white-colored door was now a dingy black. "Hey, girl!" Kaneatra said with her raspy voice. "Come on in."

Her house was always dark and creepy-looking. She was always watching some scary movie on Movie Macabre with Elvira, Mistress of the Dark. The lights were never on and the house was beyond cluttered with perpetual junk everywhere — dirty clothes and trash, ashtrays filled to the brim with cigarettes butts, plates with old dried-up food scraps, and empty or half-full alcohol bottles. A blue funk of stale cigarettes and alcohol hung in the air.

"Hey, Seanette, come give Auntie Kaneatra a hug and kiss." Seanette hugged her and then quickly scanned the living room. This was the very first thing she would do upon entering a room, looking for clues like a private investigator. Maybe, just maybe, this time her mother would pick up on her nervous, vigilant body language. Unfortunately, Pam didn't. She just sat down on the couch. Seanette sat down right next to her at the same time, like they were Siamese twins joined at the hip. "Seanette, go on in the room." She let out a heavy sigh, dropping her head looking at the carpet as she slowly walked to the room. "Audrey, Tina and Oliver are back there," Kaneatra coaxed her. "Yeah, Seanette, go on in the room," Pam chimed in. Pam taught Seanette at a very young age to always respect her and all adults. So Seanette did what she was told, got up and slowly walked out of the room.

As she made her way down the hallway, Seanette resumed the dialogue with herself. "What does Pam see in Kaneatra?" she wondered. The house was always so nasty and dirty. There were roaches everywhere, and they even had rats. She hated to use their bathroom because it always reeked of urine and the filthy toilet sometimes had feces in it. Plus, Kaneatra frequently ran out of toilet paper, so Seanette had to drip dry. The sink was eroded and the mirrors had a layer of foggy, dusty grime on them. It was so disgusting, Seanette had learned to set some ground rules for herself. She never sat on the toilet and she only urinated, waiting until she returned home to release her bowels. Sometimes it would be many hours and even days before she would rid herself of body waste, which made it very uncomfortable by the time she could.

Seanette continued down the hallway. The entire house was so dark, she felt blind. It felt like the longest walk of her life, like she had been given a death sentence that was about to be carried out.

Audrey, Oliver and Tina shared a bedroom, which always reeked of funk and musty dirty clothes. Audrey was the oldest and was ten years older than Seanette, who was nine. Like McKenna, she liked doing Seanette's hair. However, she never molested Seanette. Not herself, anyway. She actually actively encouraged her brother to do it. On a regular basis, she made statements like, "Girl, you know what Oliver want. You better give him some." Like it was joke. But no one ever contested it. They all just went along with the program. Furthermore, to Seanette's knowledge, Audrey didn't know that Tina, their baby sister, was also molesting her.

Oliver was six years older than Seanette. He was very quiet and very sneaky. His abusive interactions with her were non-verbal—she knew by the way he looked at her what he wanted, and in her self-loathing, she gave it to him with no questions asked. Oliver's sexual abuse of her was a lot different than Rashad's. Rashad brainwashed her into believing he cared about her feelings, while Oliver was a vulture. He just attacked her. He never kissed her, never played any games with her, never held a conversation with her, and they had no common interests. And yet, she was still drawn to him.

Tina was different. Tina, who was three years older than Seanette, always wanted to play games with her. She liked to play school where Seanette was always the teacher and she was the student. Tina would tell Seanette how pretty she was and how nice she looked in her clothes. In this way, Seanette felt Tina loved and accepted her, and she loved Tina, too. And like she did with McKenna, Seanette felt she owed Tina because Tina gave her so much attention.

Strangely, all of the predators in Seanette's life up to this point told her the same thing: "You think you better than me." She internalized that to the point that she sacrificed whatever part of her body would make them think and feel otherwise about her.

Seanette finished her mental conversation with herself and entered the bedroom. Audrey and Tina were sitting on the bed playing the board game Operation. Seanette loved this game. She had it when she lived in Leimert Park but, like everything else, it got stolen. Audrey allowed Seanette to play for a little while, but then signaled for her to go into the closet with Oliver. Seanette wanted to run out the door, but she remembered her mother's instruction to go back there.

Reluctantly, Seanette went into the closet. It had two entries with swinging doors. One door opened to the kids' room and the other door led to the kitchen. Inside was a mountain of dirty clothes that smelled horrible. As he usually did, Oliver was hiding under the clothes waiting for Seanette. She opened the door and walked in. As she climbed over the clothes pile, she saw Oliver moving underneath. He emerged like the Loch Ness Monster and threw Seanette on top of the pile. Seanette did not fight him off. She just assumed the position. She closed her eyes and daydreamed of her safe haven with the butterflies.

As Oliver yanked Seanette's jeans and underwear down, she took a deep breath and inhaled the perfumed scent from the flowers she had escaped to. He pulled down his pants and put his penis in the crack of her buttocks. She ran barefooted through the grass, noticing the grass blades tickling her feet. He rubbed himself aggressively against her. She saw a waterfall and ran as fast as she could towards it. He used his saliva, all the while forcing her face into those filthy clothes. The water was clear, crystal clear . . . a sea blue color. She looked down at her reflection, unfurled her wings and took flight alongside the butterflies.

After Oliver relieved himself, he told Seanette to wait for him to leave the closet first. She lay in there on top of the dirty clothes, confounded. Audrey soon interrupted Seanette's thoughts. She opened the closet door and told her to come out. Seanette sat on the bed and waited for her mother, while Audrey, Oliver and Tina all carried on like nothing happened. They ignored Seanette, as if she wasn't even in the room. Later that evening, Pam came to the door and told Seanette they would be spending the night.

Seanette was so dejected, she felt the knot in her stomach grow and harden. She just wanted to go to Joy's house. She closed her eyes and imagined Joy singing in the church about God. She kept envisioning Joy's smile until she felt Joy's spirit with her. She wanted to hold on to this vision forever. All her fears, worries and concerns seemed to disappear instantly.

"Hey, Seanette, you wanna walk to the donut shop?" This time, her thoughts were disrupted by the sound of Tina's voice. Seanette needed to quiet this pain, so she went with Tina to the donut shop and bought a lemon jelly donut and a glazed twist.

When they came back, Oliver and Audrey were in the kitchen making fried lunchmeat sandwiches. They offered Seanette a sandwich, but she declined. As the afternoon turned into evening, Pam was still not ready to leave, not until the traffic died down, she told Seanette. As Seanette walked down the dark hallway, she heard Betty Wright blaring from Kaneatra's stereo. When she returned to the kids' room, it appeared as if no one was there. Then she saw the covers on the bed moving.

Tina popped her head out. Seanette froze. She felt the knot in her stomach tighten and she became nauseous. "Come here and give me some of that," Tina said to her. Immediately, Seanette tried to daydream about home. Her home. Her safe place she created. She wanted to take flight with the butterflies, but thoughts of fear impeded her imaginary escape. Her wings were trapped. She tried to flutter them faster and faster, but to no avail. She was horrified. Tina grabbed Seanette's arm and gave her a "love" tap on her butt. Seanette was in a vortex, lost and alone.

Tina told Seanette how good she looked in her jeans. Seanette tried to fight, but Tina told her not to struggle. It was dark and hot under the blanket. Tina snatched off Seanette's shirt. She was not gentle, didn't even want to play a game first this time, and she wasn't nice. She violently pushed herself on Seanette, scratching and biting her bare, under-developed chest. Seanette tried to get out, only for Tina to say, "Stop playing hard-to-get." All Seanette could think about was her pocketbook. She closed her eyes tight. "I can't lose my pocketbook!" Tina went straight towards it. "This is my fault," Seanette kept thinking to herself. "I made her angry. I must fix it. I don't want her to be mad." Tina asked Seanette if she was enjoying what she was doing to her, but Seanette could not speak. She just kept thinking, "Why are you mad at me?" Then Seanette heard a noise. Tina was startled. Seanette's heart skipped a beat.

"Oh, God," she thought, "Please be Momma? Let her come and see for herself what they are really like behind closed doors." Tina started to back off. During this interruption, Seanette closed her legs and shut them tight together. She squeezed both her hands over her pocketbook together, determined to cover the entry to the only place that hadn't been defiled. But Pam was nowhere in sight. Tina resumed her assault. She yanked Seanette's arms and pinned her down while using her own knee as a tool to pry open Seanette's legs. All the time, she was demanding Seanette's pocketbook, telling her it belonged to her. In that moment, the love Seanette once felt for Tina turned to hatred. The next morning, Pam and Seanette drove home. Seanette never uttered a word to her mother about Tina, Oliver or Audrey.

Pam and Seanette continued to go down to Los Angeles on the weekends, to get some time away from CeCe and Teresa, but it was quite some time before they went Kaneatra's house again. In fact, Seanette had pretty much forgotten about them, because she spent most of her time at Joy's house. On one of these drives on the freeway to Los Angeles, Pam asked where Seanette would like to go and Seanette said, "Joy's house." Imagine her shock when her mother pulled up to Kaneatra's house.

Kaneatra greeted Pam and Seanette with her signature raspy salutations. By now, a lot of things had changed, much to Seanette's relief. She listened as Kaneatra told Pam the latest updates about her kids. Audrey had moved out and had a baby by a drug dealer. Oliver had been in and out of juvenile hall for petty theft and robbery. Tina had physically matured and started dating drug dealers, drinking, smoking weed and having sex with boys. Seanette sat there in disbelief. She really didn't know how to respond. Actually, while she felt some sense of relief, she also felt a bit of loss, like she had missed a big chunk of their lives. She was sad and confused at the same time.

As usual, before Seanette could get too comfortable, Kaneatra told her to go in the kids' room. But this time she added, "I don't know if Tina is back there, but you can go on in there." Seanette's immediate reaction was rejection as she picked back up on that ongoing mental dialogue with herself. "Don't know if Tina is back there? What did she mean she didn't know if she was back there? You mean I am going to be all alone? What would I do by myself?" As she walked down that long, dark hallway, so many thoughts consumed her mind as she pondered all the things Kaneatra had updated her mother on. "Oliver was in jail? For what? And for how long?" He didn't strike her as a thief. "And Tina having sex with boys?" Seanette had to admit to herself, she was mad and jealous. But why? When she reached the bedroom, it appeared to be empty. She sat down and waited, anxiously. What was happening?

Conversations with My Soul

I didn't tell
I didn't
I swear it was our little secret
I was loyal
I promise
I even pretended none of it really ever happened
I fantasize about being a virgin
I'll get married after college
I want to be someone's wife
I am still innocent
Oh Momma
I am afraid
The beautiful little girl whom all seemed to outwardly adore
I am so empty
So lonely
I am tired of fulfilling other people's needs
I have no idea
Who I am
Oh, God, please help me . . .

CHAPTER 15
Ball of Confusion

Pam and Seanette still lived with CeCe, as they were waiting for the subsidized housing agency to contact them. Seanette struggled to fit in at North Point. The student population was predominately Caucasian. Seanette was nine and in the fourth grade. She had hopes of things getting better since she was at a new school, but things just got progressively worse. For one, just to get to school, she had to take public transportation and then walk about two-miles uphill. She felt so ashamed and totally out of place as she saw all the kids being driven by their parents. She walked all year round, too, whether it was hot, cold, raining, or hailing, so her self-esteem was pretty much non-existent. She always looked at the ground and avoided all eye contact with people. Fortunately, she had a small handful of friends with whom she felt a true connection.

They were Grace, Faith, April, Michele and Robin. Seanette also had a crush on Robert, who was in her class. Grace and Seanette's birthdays were only a few days apart. Grace, April and Robert were Caucasian, Faith was Hispanic, and Robin and Michele were Asian. Grace and Seanette became best friends, and Grace and her family welcomed Seanette over to their house and treated her as part of the family. Faith was also a best friend to Seanette. She lived with her mom and grandparents and, like Grace's family, her family welcomed Seanette with love. Seanette created fond memories at Faith's house, as well.

April and Robin were the cool, down-to-earth kids who wore the latest name brand fashions from the mall. Robin always shared her lunch with Seanette. She was just giving in that way. She had no idea that Seanette didn't always have lunch or money to eat. She was just nice to her. April always had a kind word and a smile. She was like a breath of fresh air for Seanette. She would always compliment her on something everyday. Michele had a huge scratch-and-sniff sticker collection and would trade with or even give some to Seanette.

Robert had freckles and fire engine red hair. He wasn't interested in Seanette at all, but that did not stop her from liking him. The entire fourth grade knew of her enormous crush on him. She wrote his name on her notebook and always tried to talk and play with him on the logs at recess.

Seanette was so grateful for these classmates, and none of them had any idea about everything that was going on in her home environment. In no time, she acclimated herself with their dialect, clothing style and demeanor. She even wore her hair like them.

Still, she continued to struggle at North Point. She didn't feel she was good enough, nor did she feel accepted by the most of the student body. She also struggled academically; she just did not understand math. Despite staying in at recess for extra help and her friends doing what they could, she just couldn't get it. Her mother was not happy about this at all. She felt Seanette was just not applying herself. Her approach was always a whoopin.'

Pam was still using PCP, drinking and snorting, and had started freebasing cocaine with Linda on a regular basis. Linda had come back into the picture after she lost custody of her son Hakeem, who now lived with Linda's mother. Seanette was glad she didn't have to worry about him being back in the picture, too. But a whole new problem came along when her mother started dating another guy from high school named Bobby. Bobby smoked Sherm and drank heavily. He was decent to Seanette, but he only came around when he was high or wanted to get her mother high. He was another enabler. Seanette hated him.

It had been almost a year since Seanette had seen her father. And then Joy called Pam out of the blue one day and told her Sean came by her church and left a number for Seanette to reach him. He wanted to see her. Pam had some gas money, so she dropped Seanette off at Joy's house for the weekend.

Seanette was ecstatic! She yearned for her father. She adored her father. She literally worshipped the ground he walked on and believed every word that came out of his mouth. Unfortunately, what she did not know was that Sean was still wrapped up in his addiction and had in fact gotten progressively worse. He had been to jail a few times for possession of narcotics and was also homeless or "always in transition." He was increasingly unpredictable and hardly kept his word. As time went on, his visits became less frequent until it got to the point where he would never show up. Seanette would sit on Joy's couch and stare out the front window waiting for him. The few and far between times he did appear would give her hope that one day he would take her away, just like he promised. But that day never came.

This time, though, Sean did show up. Pam dropped Seanette off and told her, like always, she would be back on Sunday after church. Not long after she left, Sean arrived. Seanette was so pleased, but it didn't take her long to pick up that something had drastically changed with him. He was under the influence! She didn't know what it was, but she knew it wasn't marijuana or beer. Sean also had a lady in the car who was clearly drunk. Seanette was shocked! Her father always kept his cool and maintained control. Now, whatever this new drug was had control over him. Seanette felt the knot in her stomach tighten. He wasn't cool anymore. She wasn't mesmerized or impressed by him anymore. She was disturbed by his behavior. She was annoyed and perturbed. But she went with him anyway.

Sean had promised to take Seanette school shopping, but they spent most of the time driving around and making stops. He and his girlfriend kept getting in and out of the car, telling Seanette they were stopping at a friend's house. Each time he pulled up to an apartment complex, he told her to wait in the car and promised they would be "right back." Soon, nighttime came and Seanette was exhausted, cold and hungry, and it was time to call it a night. To her surprise, her father pulled into a motel. Apparently, he had lost his apartment and was living there with his girlfriend, who was a prostitute. Sean made it clear to Seanette that this lady was "the one." He also promised this woman was going to make him some money for the night, so he could take Seanette school shopping the next day. He never introduced the lady to Seanette; he only referred to her as "Chicken Head." They left Seanette alone in the car again, saying he would be back after he cleaned up the motel. Seanette fell asleep waiting for him. Finally, a few hours later, he returned. He woke her up and carried her from the back seat. Seanette was shivering and her teeth were chattering.

When they got into the motel room, Sean told Chicken Head to draw Seanette a bath. Seanette was afraid to take off her clothes. She did not know Chicken Head, who only smiled a lot but said very few words. Chicken Head filled the bathtub with hot water and bubbles, and then stepped out of the bathroom after telling Seanette to undress and get in the tub. Seanette disrobed and quickly got in. The water felt nice and warm to her frozen body.

After a few moments, Chicken Head returned to the bathroom and immediately, Seanette pulled the bubbles to cover her chest. Chicken Head tried to reassure her there was nothing to be afraid of. She lathered up the wash towel and washed Seanette's back. She then complimented Seanette on her hair. Seanette felt the knot in her stomach tighten. She focused on the black-and-white tile on the bathroom floor and prepared to take flight with the butterflies. Chicken Head then asked if she was hungry and Seanette said yes. Chicken Head had got her some soup and said she could eat it when she got out of the tub. Seanette then heard her father yelling for Chicken Head, who told her to enjoy her bath and the soup would be on the bed when she got out of the tub. When Seanette came out of the bathroom, the motel room was empty. She ate the soup and fell asleep. She remained alone until the next morning. That's when she told her father she was ready to go back to Joy's house.

Instantly, Sean copped an attitude. He accused Seanette of using him to get things. He then began questioning her about her mother. He asked her how everything was going. He asked if her mother was dating. He asked Seanette to tell him all the things she didn't like that her mother did. He told her she could confide in him because he "knew" something was going on, and he could feel it.

Seanette told him she didn't like living with her mother. Sean cut her off and said he knew that already. Seanette then told him she wanted to live with him. He promised her that after she told him all of how she felt, he'd make that happen. Then he asked her if she hated her mother. Seanette said she hated the way she combed her hair. Sean responded that Pam knew better because she knew Seanette was tender-headed and she shouldn't be yanking on her long, curly and thick hair. After that conversation, Seanette could not wait to get back to Joy's house because she assumed her father was going to tell her mother that their daughter was going to live with him.

Sean dropped Seanette off back at Joy's house and waited in his car for Pam to arrive. When Pam parked in the driveway and walked to the porch, Sean told Seanette to go tell her exactly how she felt. But he never got out of the car with her. Seanette was scared but mustered up the courage. While Pam and Joy were standing there on the porch, Seanette told her mother that she didn't want to live with her anymore, and that she pulled her hair too tight when she combed it.

Seanette went on to say she didn't like it when she yelled at her. She told her mother she was mean. Then Seanette told her mother she wanted to live with her father. Pam was furious. She raised her hand to hit Seanette but Joy, like always, was the gentle mediator. "Now, Pam, just calm down," she said. "Seanette, you didn't really mean those things, did you?" Seanette turned towards her father, who had now started up his car and was laughing at both her and Pam. Seanette tried to get in the car, but he drove away and left her standing there confused and devastated. As she watched him drive off from the curb, she saw that he was still laughing while he looked at her through his side view mirror.

That's when it hit Seanette. Her father had been lying to her all these years. He never had any intentions to come and get her. She could not believe it. She trusted him and he betrayed her. Why? Why didn't he want her? She wanted to run away. Her insides felt as if they were melting like wax.

Seanette knew for sure she was in for the beating of the year. Joy tried to calm Pam down, but Pam was SPITTING MAD! "You are so ungrateful. Get in the car, now! Wait 'til we get home." Seanette didn't want to go home, but she knew she had no choice.

Her mother asked her the same questions over and over all the way home, and the more she asked, the madder she got. "So, I comb your hair too tight? Yeah, you see how he pumped you up and drove off? He just manipulated your mind." Manipulate. That was the first time Seanette had heard that word, but it wasn't the last. "See?" Pam continued. "Don't you see what he is trying to do? He is tearing us apart." "Why would he want to tear us apart?" Seanette was thinking, of course, to herself. Pam wasn't done. "He had no intentions of taking you with him. Didn't you see the way he drove off and left you standing there?" Seanette thought, again to herself, "How could I not see the way he drove off? He didn't even say goodbye." As her mother continued fuming the entire ride home, Seanette just stared out the window and daydreamed. She wished she were dead. She felt blank, just empty. Oh, and manipulated.

By the time they got back to CeCe's house, Pam thought up the perfect punishment. She didn't whoop Seanette, as Seanette naively anticipated. Instead, the following morning, she made Seanette wash, comb and blow-dry her own hair all by herself. Seanette cried and begged her momma to help her, but she refused. "Don't you remember?" she mocked. "I pull your hair too tight." It ended up being an all-day fiasco. It was well into the afternoon before Pam finally gave in and helped her. Needless to say, her mother's punishment aside, Seanette no longer felt the same way about her father. She still loved him, but she lost a lot of respect for him. And yet, secretly, she did still hope one day he would come to rescue her.

Children Are Playing

Running up and down the court
The ball is elevating high. Higher! Almost! Almost . . .
Oh, no! Rebound!
The handball game is starting
I'm first! No! I am! I called it!
Feel the excitement of the carefree spirit.
Do you remember?
Red Light?
Green Light?
Mother May I?
Simon Says . . . ?
1, 2 and 3, You're Out?
Hopscotch?
Yeah! You guessed it!
See the laughter, Cinderella dressed in yellow . . .
Will someone please... jump with me?

CHAPTER 16
From Bad to Worse

Finally! Pam received her subsidized housing voucher from a government agency. Seanette was so relieved. She could not wait for it to be just her and her mother again. Maybe her mother would change once they moved. Pam packed up the Plymouth and they headed from Van Nuys to a two-bedroom apartment in Arleta. She was still unemployed, so to supplement her income, she received AFDC and food stamps. She also had a lot of spare time on her hands and started making frequent trips to her friend Debbie's house in Los Angeles.

At this stage, Seanette just went with the program. She was now a confused eleven-year-old girl with no identity, who just went with the wind. She felt she was living a double life, too. During the week, she was at school with all her diverse, well-off friend, attending chapel and Bible classes. Then, on the weekends, she was in the inner city, on the east side of Los Angeles, in the depths of the ghetto, where drugs, gang violence and poverty surrounded her. This was very confusing to her because she felt she didn't fit in anywhere. But that was nothing new for her. Seanette was so numb. She had even stopped daydreaming about her homeland with the butterflies, waterfalls, blue skies and perfect sunshine. She adapted to this double life as her "normal," but her mind was in a constant unsettled state.

When Pam and Seanette pulled up to Debbie's house, it was usually inevitable that they would be spending the night. Seanette no longer asked to go over Joy's house. Besides the fact that Pam regularly said she didn't have enough gas money, Seanette was beginning to wonder if God was punishing her or if He was angry with her. She could not grasp a logical reason why her life had so much turmoil and trauma or why her parents were the way they were. Seanette started to get resentful and angry at God, so she no longer wanted to go to church or any church activities.

When Pam and Seanette pulled up to Debbie's, Seanette saw Wana, Ty and the neighborhood kids playing outside. She joined them while her mother went in the house. As soon as Seanette got out of the car, she heard the girls singing made-up cheers, "Jump in the car, put your foot on the gas, step back, and let Wana pass." That led to, "Sitting at the table, peeling my potatoes, waiting for the clock to boom tick, tock, boom tick, eollie, ollie." ·

These girls were also incredible dancers and, of course, were great at jump rope. If there were no real jump ropes, they used water hoses or extension cords. Seanette loved to jump rope but Double Dutch was always a challenge for her. So, she just turned the double ropes for the other girls and sang all the songs as they jumped. Now, the one game she could beat everybody at was handball. Seanette was the handball queen. Since she always won, she got to pick all the rules. She only allowed one lifesaver, no pop-ups, waterfalls, everlasting slices, babies — oh, and no friendships.

The two questions everyone in the neighborhood asked about Seanette were, "Where did she come from?" and "How does Wana know her?" They noticed that Seanette's mannerisms, etiquette, style of dress, physical features and the texture of her hair were completely opposite from Wana's. Now, Wana had an answer for everything, and when she didn't, she made things up. She told everyone in her neighborhood that she and Seanette were real sisters and they had the same father who only allowed her to visit in the summer or on selected weekends. This gave Seanette a sense of belonging. She knew the kids feared Wana, which to Seanette was a plus. She figured no one would try to beat her up or treat her too badly because, after all, she was Wana's "sister."

Wana was two years younger than Seanette, but she was very knowledgeable about drugs and sex. Unlike Seanette, Wana had already started her menstruation, at nine years old. She had short-coiled hair that was balding on the sides, and her clothes and shoes were worn out and tattered. She got teased a lot about everything, from her looks to her house to her mother's physical appearance. The neighborhood kids even made up mean songs about her. Before long Wana became known as a bully for fighting because she would fight anybody, she didn't care. She fought kids bigger than her and smaller than her. She fought the kids making fun of her or just because she didn't like them. Mostly, she fought kids who talked about her, her brother or her mother. Wana demanded respect.

The neighborhood kids made fun of Debbie because she was a large woman, about six-two and almost four hundred pounds. She kept a rag or bandana on her head because she never combed her hair, nor did she ever groom her full-grown beard. She rarely wore a bra under her old, ratted, holey muumuus. The soles of her large feet were stained permanently black because she hardly wore shoes, and her heels had cracks that resembled cracks in a sidewalk. And her house was as filthy as Kaneatra's, Pam's other friend.

Debbie, Wana and Ty lived in a house owned by relatives, who allowed her to live there with her children. Seanette spent many summers with them, and their house became her second home. She knew everyone and played with the neighborhood kids.

A Letter for My Dad

I thought about putting some words
Together on a notepad
After procrastinating, I jotted down the words
A letter for My Dad
I reflect on how you would pop up in and out of my life
Broken dreams and promises filled my mind with spite
There were those times when you did show up
Said you could take me away from my mother
In those times of heartache
I question did you ever love me or her
I only felt close to you when you gave me food
Or got me high
Just a temporary fix and you never said goodbye
You told me you were proud of me when
I got straight A's in school
Being perfect in my mind
Was my only tool
I stared deeply in your eyes
As you promised to always be there
In my unspoken silence
My heart cries
This is so unfair
You overcompensated
Because of guilt and shame
I never spoke out
It was myself I blamed
This pain so deep
I can't quite grasp to explain
I hated to carry not only your last

But also part of your first name
Why should I carry someone's name
who showed no love
To feel or see
This little girl inside just wants to know
Why you abandoned me
Your smile to me was priceless
You swore to get things back on track
I swear I never doubted
I always had your back
I began to search for clues
I wanted to know for myself the news
I met up close and personal
Actually stumbled into
Your new friend
You see
Dad
When you found cocaine
You lost me in the end

CHAPTER 17

Flying High

It was a crisp fall afternoon when Seanette answered the phone. "Hello?" "Hey, I have a belated birthday present for you, Baby Cakes, but make sure you and your mom come by my apartment at nighttime. It has to be today and has to be at nighttime." Sean spoke with such serious intensity his voice. The call was strange to her, but she wanted to see what the urgency was. After she begged to go to Los Angeles, Pam drove Bobby's maroon Ford Mustang. When they arrived at the address Sean provided, he was standing outside.

They hardly recognized him. He was terribly thin. He made a beeline to the car to tell them to turn the engine off and wait, then he disappeared for a second and came right back . . . with a ten-speed bike. A used, stolen bike. He quickly loaded it into Pam's trunk and told her to hurry and drive away. Seanette could not believe it. A stolen bike? What was he thinking? That was it for her. She told herself from that day forward, the man she knew as her father no longer existed. In her mind, he was dead.

When they returned home, Pam and Bobby got into a huge fight. Seanette was glad when they broke up. Pam kicked him out after finding out he cheated on her with his ex-wife. Once again, Seanette thought she could finally have her mother all to herself. But that was not the case.

The longest period of time that Pam and Seanette lived in their home alone was between four and six months, maximum. Even if no one lived with them, people were always hanging out there or visiting "for a spell." At one point, Pam's friend Linda had gotten kicked out of her place and had nowhere to live, so Pam allowed her to live with them.

Initially, Linda was barely there because she was always at her boyfriend's house. Soon, she was always at the apartment with her friends and they all, including Pam, would be up all night getting high. Pam had started working as a receptionist but soon stopped going to work. Oftentimes, Seanette would come home and find her there with Linda and her friends, high. Seanette also found cocaine residue on the bathroom counter, along with burnt cotton swabs that had been dipped in alcohol, to be used as torches for the homemade pipe for freebasing.

Pam's personality drastically changed. For one thing, she started stealing food from the grocery store when they didn't have any at home. Initially, she'd only steal flavored drink packets. Progressively, the list grew to bottles of seasonings, and then to meats and other items. She would order hot food items from the deli, like chicken wings, and eat them in the store before she would have to pay for them. "If you eat it in the store, it's not stealing" was her motto. She had become a professional shoplifter and Seanette hated going to the store with her, she was so embarrassed. Pam would have her go to different aisles to get things to steal and even had her stuff the items in her purse. Pam didn't care if people were in the aisle or watching.

One day they finally got caught. They were on their way walking out of the store when two security guards stopped them at the door. The men told Seanette to wait in the aisle by the freezer section while they escorted Pam to the back of the store. Seanette anxiously paced the floor. "Oh no, not again." She thought her mother was going to jail. Eventually, the security guards let Pam go because the value of everything she had stolen didn't exceed two hundred dollars.

Seanette was overwhelmed with so many emotions, but her mother didn't seem to feel anything. She just simply remained quiet as they walked back to the apartment empty-handed. To make matters worse, when they did return, their lights and phone had been turned off. Plus, they had no toilet paper or other toiletries. Agitated, Pam showed Seanette how to rub newspaper together until it got soft and how not to overuse the dishwashing liquid. Beyond those moments of agitation, her attitude was entirely apathetic and detached toward these problems. It seemed she couldn't care less, just as long as her drug habit was being provided for.

There was only one option left. Call Diane. This responsibility was always left up to Seanette. Every time ends didn't quite meet, Pam waited for Seanette to think to call Diane. Things could be totally out of control, but Pam would never call her herself. Seanette had to do it. Thankfully, Diane never turned them away when they needed food. Usually, she would pick up Seanette after work and take her to the grocery store, or just drop by with groceries.

Seanette preferred Diane to drop the groceries off as opposed to going to the store with her because, if she had to go, the conversation was always the same. Diane wanted to know why they didn't have any food, spewing out an endless line of derogatory questions. For this reason, Seanette wouldn't tell her what was really going on. She just simply lied. She took upon herself the responsibility to always cover for her mother because she didn't want anyone to know Pam was on drugs, and she was afraid of her. Besides, her mother had conditioned her to second-guess herself, that she was completely crazy and had only imagined all the things she had seen or heard.

Needless to say, a trip with Diane to the grocery store was both relieving and stressful at the same time for Seanette. Relieving, because it meant she and her mother would have the food and other things they desperately needed. Stressful, because of Diane's attitude and her mother's short temper. Diane went down every aisle in the store, naming off items asking, "You got this? You got that?" Seanette always hesitated in answering because, first of all, she was scared her mother would be mad at her if she answered wrong. Second, she didn't like how Diane usually responded. Diane was angry and harsh and said mean things about both of them. Diane especially badmouthed Pam, which really hurt and angered Seanette. Third, Seanette felt dumb, confused and embarrassed, which caused her to always respond with a low, muffled "No" and Diane would just roll her eyes and retort back, "Well, what have you been using?" Seanette didn't have the heart or guts to tell her they've been using newspaper. Fourth, although Diane was always willing to buy school clothes and supplies and food, or even to give pocket money, she always made Seanette feel like she owed her for it. Still, Seanette had to deal with whatever Diane dished out, because they needed her help.

Seanette was only allowed to go over to Diane's on Sundays, in order to go to church. Pam's Aunt Regina, Desi and Angel would take Seanette with them and if Regina's car wasn't running, Diane took everybody. Diane's house was always clean. Her kitchen was stocked with all the food and goodies a kid could ever want or think of, and there was cable television in every room. Pam never went to Diane's. She either stayed home or went to Los Angeles. So, Seanette always brought her mother food back from the Sunday dinners Diane prepared.

Diane started working overtime on Sundays, so the trips to her house became less frequent. Seanette started spending a lot of her Sundays at home with her buddies—the refrigerator and the television—while her mother was gone to Los Angeles. Seanette developed her own routine. First, she would clean up the house, and then she would watch popular sitcoms that all came on the same channel. In between the commercials, she would fix different snacks out of whatever food was there. She stopped calling Diane when they needed food, because she didn't want to deal with her negative comments and derogatory attitude. So, she became creative with her meals, learning to make something out of nothing. For instance, if they didn't have bread, she used saltine crackers or tortillas.

Even though Seanette was never taught how to cook, she had watched others and even experimented on her own. This is how she learned to make sugar bread, from watching Oliver and Tina at their house when she was younger. She really liked sugar bread. It was a great substitute for sweets and was easy to make since it was simply sandwich bread (preferably white) spread with margarine and sprinkled with lots of sugar, and then put in the oven or broiler. She next learned how to make fried potatoes, which became her specialty.

Seanette really enjoyed cooking and eating. Anytime was a good time for her to eat. She would fantasize about food, and overeating was second nature for her. She ate until her stomach hurt. She would eat even if she wasn't hungry, basically just because it tasted good.

This Numb Feeling

Makes everything non-existent
No concerns, worries or fears
It brings a rollercoaster ride filled
With drama and tears
It feeds off insecurities
Gives the illusion that everything is okay
Huh?
It didn't start out that way
At first, this numb feeling shared its joy
Protection from all hurt and pain
Reliable to the end
Closest, dearest, most trusted friend
Never took the time to recognize
This numb feeling
Took up
Too much time
Lost souls searching
To find
This numb feeling

CHAPTER 18

Spiraling Out of Control

Pam's addiction began to get significantly worse. She regularly smoked Sherm and snorted and smoked cocaine. Alcohol had become a problem for her, as well. Seanette hoped a nearly fatal incident they experienced together would cause her mother to come to her senses.

One morning while Pam was driving her to school, they came upon big semi-truck that was blocking the street. When Pam pressed the brake pedal, the car refused to stop. No brakes! Seanette was scared but, for a moment, she wanted to die. She was ready to leave this entire horrible world behind. What a better way to die than with her momma where she could finally have her to herself? Of course, that wasn't her mother's thought. As Pam desperately held her foot on that brake pedal, she suddenly grabbed Seanette's hand and started to pray. It immediately brought to Seanette's mind how everything was when she and her momma used to go to church together. In that instant, her hope was restored, and she began to pray, too. The car screeched to a halt literally seconds away from colliding with the truck! Mother and daughter let out a simultaneous "Thank You, Jesus!"

This brush with death gave Seanette high hopes that her mother would get her life together. Sadly, things only got worse. Even though they lived in the same apartment, Pam and Seanette hardly interacted. When they did, it was always confrontational. Pam was increasingly withdrawn and violent towards Seanette, losing her patience and being easily irritated even for things that were beyond Seanette's control. Seanette got hit for everything. If they had no food, her mother hit her.

If Pam was mad at someone else, she took it out on her. At any given time, Pam would grab Seanette by her hair and throw her to the ground.

At some point, to Seanette's disappointment, Pam abruptly kicked Linda out for stealing some belongings. Seanette had mixed feelings about it because Linda was nice to her. Besides the fact that she was so pretty with a cocoa complexion and perfect, extra-white teeth, she let Seanette play in her makeup. Pam would have whooped her if she had known. Seanette was well aware that Linda was on drugs and was the cause of a lot of problems, but she truly believed that Linda could, and would, help her if given a chance.

Seanette still struggled with her studies at North Point, especially math. Pam assumed it was because she wasn't trying, thinking Seanette just sat there. The truth was, Seanette simply didn't understand. At one point, Pam did find her a tutor. He was an older white man who lived across town and Seanette had to take the bus by herself to get there since they no longer had a car. She always felt intimidated while at his house. Although he never tried anything, being there triggered Seanette's major trust issues, which, in turn, hindered her ability to learn and understand math.

Of course, Pam didn't know about those trust issues because Seanette never told her about all of the abuse she endured. In any event, Pam was livid about Seanette's lack of progress even with the tutoring and, soon enough, Seanette stopped going. She continued to get bad grades in math, and Pam continued to whoop her or curse her out for it. That was Pam's answer. "Sooner or later, you will get tired of getting whoopin's," she'd always say.

Compounding the problem was that Seanette had come to resent the school. She just did not fit in. All the kids' parents were well off and the kids were all trendy. Plus, Seanette was a latchkey kid, at home by herself until her mother got home. Not to mention, she was the only black student in the entire school.

Meanwhile, Pam made new friends, Kathy and her sister Lucy, who conveniently lived right around the corner. Kathy had two daughters. Jennifer was about four years older than Seanette, and Shelia was eleven years old, same age as Seanette.

Jennifer and Shelia were very mature for their ages. They wore makeup and fake nails, and they both were fully developed and sexually active. They attended the nearby public junior high and high schools and were very vocal to Pam that she should put Seanette in public school with them.

Shelia was the neighborhood bully. She always made fun of Seanette's undeveloped body, calling her "flat-chested." She also taunted her because of her complexion, calling her "Spook" or "Burnt Toast, "and she called her a "bald-headed Indian chief" because she didn't have any hair under her arms. Seanette hated to be around them. But, like always, she had no choice, because her mom and their mom got high together. Neither Jennifer nor Shelia tried to molest her, but the unrelenting bullying, taunting and verbal abuse was just as bad.

The common bond between Pam, Kathy and Lucy was all about cocaine. Kathy freebased, period, and she preferred it in rock form. She snorted cocaine when she had to, or smoked marijuana. Lucy didn't really like to freebase. She "paperbased," or smoked "primos," which was cocaine mixed in a marijuana joint. She also smoked "coco puffs," or "puffs," which was cocaine mixed into a cigarette. Pam smoked coco puffs and primos with Kathy and Lucy, and was pretty careless about it. Quite often, Seanette found pieces of cigarettes torn open with cocaine residue inside, or razor blades and cut up pieces of drinking straws with cocaine left on them. Her mother would leave these things either on the table or on a saucer pushed under the couch, which Seanette usually found while cleaning up the house.

Kathy also had a dealer who called himself "Bandit." He was a short and slick-looking man who wore the latest name-brand clothes and who everybody thought was drop-dead gorgeous. Except Seanette. He repulsed her. She knew what he was: just another fiend like her mother's ex-husband Damon. She could not understand how he had no problem making house deliveries and socializing with the kids in the home.

Just like when Pam and Seanette lived in Los Angeles, the drug parties were usually held at their place and lasted all night. One day, when Seanette came home from school, she discovered Pam had not gone to work.

When she opened the door, she saw a strange man there, sitting on the couch with her mother, who was clearly in a serious comatose, zombie-like state. As Seanette walked in, her eyes were drawn to this big glass pipe in the middle of the table, along with a bottle of rubbing alcohol and cotton balls. Seanette was familiar with this scene. It was obvious her mother had been freebasing and this man was no doubt the supplier. Seanette went off on the man and demanded he leave. He refused at first, but then Pam was finally able to speak and, with noticeable reluctance, told him he had better go. Seanette was incredulous and fuming! Why was he hesitating to leave? And why was her mother acting like she really didn't want him to go?

The man tried to explain to Seanette that her mother was all right. He put on his shoes, gathered his paraphernalia and, as he stood up to leave, told Pam he would "see her later." "Yeah, right," Seanette thought to herself as he walked out the door. Her mother then tried to tell Seanette that she had an allergic reaction to some medication, but Seanette knew better.

At this point, though, she was very scared. Her mother's eyes were completely yellow and darting around. That's when Pam told Seanette to pray with her. She told her to get her Bible and read Psalm 23 out loud. Seanette was crying, and so was Pam. "I'm sorry, I'm sorry," she kept saying to her daughter.

After that day, Pam stopped hanging with Kathy, but she became very close with Lucy and also met a new friend to get high with. Cecelia was young and beautiful, but she loved cocaine. Snorting and smoking it was her preference. She bragged about hanging out and getting high with famous people. She also knew Bandit and many other dealers. She and Lucy were over to the apartment at least three nights on the weekdays and every weekend.

Pam and Lucy often went out to nightclubs, and one night they got arrested for possession of cocaine. Pam was in jail for a weekend but because she had less than a gram, it was not enough to hold her. She told Seanette that the police had found Seanette's Paris doll's air freshener and thought it was cocaine. Seanette did not say a word, but she didn't own any Paris air freshener.

After that, Pam did make some improvement with her drug habit. She started to decrease her dependence on PCP, and it wasn't long before she stopped smoking it altogether. Seanette took this as a sign that her substance abuse was coming to an end. Another sign was that her mother started spending more positive, quality time with her. They often watched television and movies together.

Seanette was convinced these changes were because God was answering her prayers. She had stopped going to church with Joy, mainly because they didn't have a car. So, she went to a neighborhood church for a while with her cousins Desi and Angel. By now, Desi was driving, so she took them every week. This church, like everything else, was a culture shock to Seanette. Everything was different. The majority of the congregation was white, and their form of worship, preaching and prayer time was totally different from the Baptist church Seanette grew up in. Still, she enjoyed going.

The pastor was a reserved man who taught the Bible like a teacher in a classroom. He didn't groan and grunt the way the reverend did when the spirit hit. The praise songs were displayed on an overhead projector, not in a hymn book. At the Baptist church, the deacons did devotions, but here everyone collectively sang praises in the spirit. The offering time was just simply passing plates down the aisles, whereas in the Baptist church, the entire congregation walked around the church while gospel music played.

The biggest difference to Seanette was prayer time. At her old church, if you needed prayer, everyone came down to the altar at once and sang a song while holding hands with their eyes closed. Then, they remained silent as the reverend prayed out loud with a general prayer. At this church, the pastor instructed everyone to partner up with four people whom you did not know, tell each other your prayer requests, and then take turns praying out loud for each need.

Seanette was certain her mother would change with this much prayer power. She was always eager to get to that part of the service because she expected to see the results when she got home. Surely, God heard her now. She strongly believed that, since adults were praying with her and for her mother, things would have to change. After all, they knew how to really pray. Her prayer was always the same: "Please, God, help my mom stop using drugs." So, when Pam stopped using Sherm, Seanette was elated. She thought God had finally answered her prayers.

But then Seanette started to struggle with her prayer life. She didn't know how to approach God, especially because her mother wasn't really changing and, in fact, was getting worse. Pam had quit Sherm, but her dependence on cocaine, marijuana and alcohol increased. And so did the beatings. All this made Seanette start blaming God. She eventually stopped praying for her mother. Truthfully, she thought God was punishing her. She felt the knot in her stomach turn. She became angry and bitter and turned her back on God.

Little Brown Girl

Little Brown Girl come outside and play
Little Brown Girl don't you dare pay
Attention to what they say
Little Brown Girl don't hang your head down
Raise your head up
Smile and pick your pride up off the ground
Little Brown Girl even when your feelings get hurt and
Sometimes you don't know what to say
Remember your destiny is greatness
In time it will be revealed someday

CHAPTER 19

Merry "Go" Round

Nineteen-eighty-six had rolled around, and Seanette made it to her twelfth birthday and to the sixth grade by the skin of her teeth. She couldn't believe that she passed fifth grade! On the weekdays, she started spending the afternoons and evenings at Auntie Regina's house, taking the city bus there because it was close to her school. Aunt Regina was really good at making sure Seanette was fed and all her homework was done before letting her play outside. She and Angel even helped Seanette with her homework. Pam would show up later in the evening, sometimes as late as ten o'clock, usually drunk, high or both. She would blow the car horn for Seanette instead of coming inside, which she never did. Seanette was always anxious about her mother's state of mind, since her behavior was so unpredictable.

Seanette was actually glad to go to Aunt Regina's house after school everyday because she could hang out with her cousin Angel instead of being home alone. Being around Angel allowed Seanette to just be a kid, like watching cartoons and playing dolls.

Plus, she really looked up to Angel, who was so independent and had enormous self-confidence! Angel knew who she was and what she liked and didn't care what other people thought or said about her. She was completely "out-the-box" and quite liberal about expressing her opinions. She was a rebel and proud of it. She was bold! She was fierce! She was strong! She was different from anyone Seanette knew. She always had big dreams and encouraged Seanette to never be scared to dream herself, regardless of what people said. Angel gave Seanette hope. She felt safe, protected, beautiful and important when Angel talked to her.

"Seanette, are you sure you aren't going to get in trouble?" Angel asked that same question every time she painted Seanette's nails and every time, Seanette lied to her because she admired her so much and didn't want to disappoint her. Seanette knew she was going to get a whoopin' but didn't care. She wanted to be like Angel. Sadly, Seanette had become rather accustomed to getting whooped for practically everything. Pam never allowed her to wear nail polish or wear her hair down in her eyes because she considered it being "fast." Angel would make designs with the nail polish, sometimes using three colors and painting stripes, and other times, dots.

In just a matter of time, Seanette felt close enough with Angel to tell her about her mother's drug addiction and the beatings. To her surprise, Angel already knew. Seanette went on to tell her in detail about the time that Pam whooped her because of a "D" on her report card for math. Pam used a thick leather belt to hit her repeatedly all over her body. In desperation, Seanette grabbed the belt and Pam demanded it back, but when Seanette noticed she was bleeding, she just panicked and froze. Pam became even more enraged! She told Seanette to keep the belt because she was going to get the extension cord. While she left for a moment, Seanette ran and locked herself in the bathroom.

At this point in the story, Angel's eyes began to well up with tears as Seanette began to shake and sob uncontrollably as she described how utterly terrified she was.

Pam started yelling and cursing, screaming louder and louder, "Open this door!" She then kicked the door in with her foot and proceeded to beat Seanette with the extension cord, forcing her into the shower and turning on the water to intensify the sting. Later, to add insult to injury, Pam blamed her for the hole in the middle of the bathroom door. She used a movie poster from Seanette's room to cover it.

Then Seanette took off her jacket to show Angel the welts and bruises. Angel was shocked and absolutely furious. That night when Pam came to pick Seanette up, Angel told her not to go outside. Pam kept honking the horn, and Seanette was scared. She knew the consequences for making her mother wait, because Pam often hit her while in the car driving if she felt Seanette took too long. By now, Auntie Regina was calling up the stairs, "Seanette, your momma is outside." But Angel stood her ground and told Seanette again not to move.

Seanette's heart was racing with thoughts both good and bad as she felt the knot in her stomach tighten. At first, a sudden a burst of hope came. "Maybe I'll get help now," she thought. "Or maybe I can live with Auntie Regina and Angel." But then sadness overwhelmed her, eclipsing those positive thoughts and reverting her back to her co-dependent, pseudo-parental role. "What about momma? Who is going to take care of her? Who is going to help her?"

Pam was beyond agitated now. She got out of the car, walked up to the house and banged on the screen door. When Regina opened it, Pam was clearly drunk and high. Angel told Seanette to stay in the room again, then she went out to the top of the stairs and, without any trepidation, boldly voiced to Pam that she needed to stop hurting Seanette and that she needed to get some help because she had a drug problem.

That brought Pam's rage to the surface and she started cursing Angel out. That's when Auntie Regina told Angel to be quiet and told Seanette to get her stuff ready to go. Now fuming herself, Angel started to cry and yell at Pam, but Seanette really had no other choice but to leave there with her mother. The entire car ride home, as Seanette sat in the back seat, her mother repeatedly reached back and socked and slapped her in the face. Because of Pam's erratic driving, Seanette flew across the backseat, so Pam made her position herself in the middle of the back seat and keep her arms folded across her chest so that she could hit her without missing.

In between blows, Pam ranted about how Seanette was turning her back on her. She scolded her about how whatever happens in the house stays in the house. Then, Pam insisted Seanette was crazy for thinking she used drugs. She denied it, saying she only had an occasional beer or joint, and that was not a bad thing.

Seanette prayed that, by the time they got home, Pam would be exhausted. But she wasn't. Once inside the house, Pam threw shoes at her, and hit her arms and legs with wooden spoons, and slapped her in the mouth—all the while continuing with the ranting and raving. Pam then beat her with an extension cord and made her get in the shower to intensify the sting.

After that horrific night, Seanette did not see Auntie Regina or Angel for about two years. Worse, as time passed, her hopes for her mother to get clean grew dimmer and dimmer. She went into a deep depression and turned more towards food as a comfort.

One day, Seanette came home from school and was greeted by her Uncle Bruce, her mother's brother. With him were his girlfriend Tanya, and her daughter Gloria. According to Pam, they were moving in. Bruce was about six years younger than Pam. He had been in the Air Force but was dishonorably discharged for stealing checks from the government.

Seanette had always been quite fond of her uncle. He always tried to bring her and Pam souvenirs from all the different countries he visited while in the military. He taught Seanette how to swim, ride her bike without the training wheels, roller-skate and cook. He would make her scrambled eggs, pancakes and fried doughnuts made out of biscuits, which she learned how to make by watching him. He also often gave her money for her birthday or just because. And when he was still stationed at the Air Force Base not too far north of Los Angeles, he sometimes took her and Pam there to look at the planes.

Once Bruce moved in, Seanette's fond memories were replaced by the devastating realization that her favorite uncle was a cocaine addict just like her mother. Bruce was always gone on binges for several days or sometimes even weeks. When he returned, he was completely out of it and slept for days, and then, once he regained his strength and ate a little bit, he was out in the streets again.

To make matters harder for young Seanette, Bruce's girlfriend Tanya was a heroin addict and an alcoholic. Plus, they argued and fist fought a lot. One time he beat her so badly, he gave her a huge black eye and a busted lip. No one intervened or said anything afterwards. Like always in Seanette's household, life just resumed.

Once Bruce, Tanya and Gloria moved in, Pam tacked on more house chores and responsibilities on Seanette. And not just any chores. She not only had to clean up the entire house by herself, she also had to wash everyone's clothes on Saturdays—about ten loads, easy. Not to mention, she had to push a shopping cart full of clothes down the street to the laundromat, then wash, dry and fold everything, and then push the cart back home. All by herself. Pam would make sarcastic statements about it, like, "The clothes will be much lighter when you're pushing them in the cart on the way back."

Even still, Seanette tried to be perfect and stay under the radar to avoid upsetting her mother, even though there was no rhyme or reason to the beatings. Pam was simply in a constant agitated state of frustration, irritability and anger. This meant that she would just hit her seemingly at the drop of a hat, and she would do it with brooms, mops, pots, shoes or whatever was within reach at that moment. And, of course, Seanette most feared another extension cord beating, especially while naked, and that follow-up shower.

Bruce, like Pam was also actively involved in fraudulent insurance schemes. One day, Pam, Bruce and Seanette went to the grocery store. Seanette accidentally slipped on some liquid and fell. Seeing an opportunity, her mother was glad! Thankfully, Seanette wasn't hurt too badly. But in the midst of this, Bruce decided to fake a fall into some wine bottles and got a bad cut on his thigh. He claimed there was some liquid left on the floor there, as well—which, of course, was hard to investigate now that the floor was covered in wine. Then, as if all that wasn't enough, Pam decided to take a shopping cart filled with groceries from a woman who was checking out nearby, using Seanette as a cover to wheel the cart to the car.

Seanette and Bruce went to physical therapy for their injuries and three months later, they were granted a settlement for their pain and suffering. But Seanette never saw any of her portion of the money. The lawyer's office misunderstood the relationship between Pam, Bruce and Seanette. Assuming that, because Pam and Bruce had the same last name, Bruce was Seanette's father, not her uncle, the lawyer released the checks from both settlements to Bruce. Needless to say, Bruce disappeared on another binge and did not return for a long time. When he finally did come back, he was so sick because he had nearly overdosed. Pam and Seanette had to nurse him back to health, with him constantly throwing up and sweating profusely at all times of the night. He apologized numerous times for stealing Seanette's money, but predictably, once he recuperated, he was back on the streets.

Eventually, Pam kicked Bruce out after he stole from her again, this time not giving her portion of the profits they were supposed to split from another one of their scams. Pam had grown tired of his shenanigans, but Seanette, like always, had mixed feelings. Still, she understood why he had go. Besides, with him, Tanya and Gloria gone, she had fewer clothes to wash.

Sweet Dreams are Made of This

A love so pure, acceptance is real
My heart is overwhelmed
By the love, joy and peace in my soul I feel
A voice so gentle
A smile so genuine and kind
A laugh so pure
A spirit that lights up any room
Finally, hopelessness and sadness no longer loom
No more endless nights of praying
Or wishing on a star
You are
A God-send
My very own Real Daddy

CHAPTER 20
Make a Wish

W hen Pam's car broke down, all visits to Los Angeles, or any where else for that matter, slowed down. Seanette was glad. Besides seeing this as God's way of freeing her from being molested, she thought it was answered prayer for Pam to get off drugs. She and her momma started spending some quality time together. Pam even let her pick the TV movies they watched. Seanette usually picked the ones that had to do with drug, physical or child abuse in hopes that her mother would get an understanding of how she felt. Pam didn't.

There was somewhat of a positive turning point, though. Pam suddenly took an interest in a neighborhood park, telling Seanette she wanted to start exercising. At first, she rode Seanette's ten-speed bike, then tried skating with Seanette's roller skates, and finally settled on walking to the park. Pam was certainly getting exercise, but Seanette had learned long ago to always suspect there was more behind her mother's motives than what her mother said. Seanette was right. Pam was going down to the park for two reasons: to buy marijuana, and she had met a man.

Christopher was his name and, happily, he was the best thing that had ever happened to them. He was the most beautiful, brilliant man, and he came to love both Pam and Seanette dearly, and they adored him. The time they shared as a family was something out of a storybook. He wasn't a womanizer, he didn't hit Pam and he didn't run the streets. More importantly, he didn't bring them down with an out-of-control drug habit. He was such a breath of fresh air.

For Seanette, Christopher was a dream come true. He was kind, thoughtful and had a gentle, million-dollar smile that gave her a fortress of comfort. He didn't pretend. He didn't lie. He had no hidden agendas. She found it hard to believe that such a genuine blessing had entered her life. Indeed, it didn't take long for her to call him "Daddy." He was a child at heart himself, and loved to play basketball or have water fights with her. Plus, he taught her how to cook meals, and even how to drive when she was still just twelve years old. She had never gotten Sean a Father's Day gift, because he was never around. But she and Pam got Christopher one, a set of Snap-On tools of his very own for his steady job as a mechanic at an auto body shop. Christopher embraced Seanette as his own and told people she was his daughter. None of Pam's boyfriends showed any interest in Seanette, not even remotely.

The most important thing Christopher did was assume the responsibility as the head of their household. With a legitimate and steady job, he was a provider who treated both Pam and Seanette like queens. At the very least, they always had food, and the phone and lights were never cut off. More than that, he invested time and energy into both of them. He drove Seanette to school so she didn't have to take the bus. He actually helped her with school work and even went to her parent-teacher conferences.

Christopher liked going places and doing things as a family, such as barbequing at the park and going to drive-in movies on the weekends. He even brought home a couple of dogs, a pit bull named Patches and a terrier named Scottie. Seanette's faith was restored in God, and she was so thankful for Christopher. She finally felt a sense of self-worth because of him.

Pam turned into a completely different person when Christopher came into their lives, seeming to let go of her self-destructive habits. She stopped whooping Seanette because Christopher became the disciplinarian and believed in talking to a child instead of hitting or yelling. If he was angry, he would just take a short walk outside and come back.

Christopher moved in with Pam and Seanette rather swiftly. Things continued to be good, at least for a while. As time passed, Seanette noticed he was starting to act a little strange. He began hanging out with Pam's friends who lived around the corner, and before long, the nighttime traffic at the house started to build up again. At first, Seanette couldn't tell if he was using drugs. She only saw him drink beer and smoke cigarettes. But soon it became very clear; Christopher had started indulging in the drug scene.

Seanette became so anxious about this, if for no other reason than that she didn't know if her mother was selling drugs again and the cops were going to bust through the door like they did once before. One thing she did know for sure was that everyone was using cocaine in the house, including Christopher. This deeply saddened her, but, as she always did, she ate her feelings away.

For a while, everything among the three of them seemly went on "as normal" for the most part. Christopher still had his job and continued in the role of head of household, while Pam got a bookkeeping job and Seanette was doing a little bit better in school. They were able to move into a bigger apartment and settled in. By this time, their pit bull Patches had run away by this time, but their terrier Scottie was like a bonus second child in the home. Everybody loved him.

Seanette received word from Joy that Sean wanted to see her and take her school shopping. As it happened, Seanette and her mother and Christopher had planned to drive out to Oceanside for the weekend to visit Christopher's sister Nancy. They often went to visit or go on family vacations with Nancy and her husband and five children, and Seanette always had such fun with them. But she still had high hopes for Sean and, despite everything, she never turned down an opportunity to see him. So, instead of going to Oceanside, she asked to be dropped off at Joy's house in Los Angeles.

It was a Friday evening and freeway traffic was packed. Throughout the entire drive, Christopher kept asking Seanette if she was sure about getting dropped off at Joy's instead of going to Oceanside. Seanette always responded, "I'm sure." She was certain that this time, her father would come through. She just knew he would make everything right, he would keep his word, he would move her away into a mansion with a maid, just like he always promised. She would get to go back to her old school when they lived in Leimert Park. She would see all of her old friends the butterflies, ladybugs and flowers, and spend time with Stacy and Tom the mailman. She would be free.

Once at Joy's, Christopher asked Seanette one more time. She looked straight into his eyes and said, yet again, "I want to stay." He left it at that and brought her suitcase to the door. Seanette turned and watched as the red brake lights glowed in the dark as he and her mother drove away.

Seanette got up bright and early the next morning. She took her bath and then helped clean the bedroom with the other kids. After the chores were done, all the kids went outside in the front yard to play. Except Seanette. She sat down on the couch and watched out the window as the cars went by, hoping that one of them would be her father.

Saturday afternoon rolled around, and Seanette was still on the couch keeping an eye out. But still no sign of her father. At one point, Joy gave all the kids a little pocket change to buy some junk food at the corner store. But Seanette didn't go with them or do anything else they were doing. She just stayed on the couch, afraid that if she went anywhere, she would miss her dad. Then, Saturday afternoon and evening came and went.

The next morning, Seanette went to church and later out to dinner with Joy, Nathan and the kids, but she couldn't wait to get back to their house. She had prayed in church that Sean would be there. As soon as they got back to Joy's house, Seanette got out of the car and went straight to her spot on the couch. She waited there for her father all the way until Christopher and Pam came to pick her up. Sean never showed up, nor did he call. Seanette felt so stupid. Once again, she was gullible enough to believe him. The knot in her stomach grew and tightened. She vowed to herself that day to never trust anyone again.

In the Blink of an Eye

In the blink of an eye
Terror and panic overtake my mind
I am helpless
I am hopeless
Searching to find
Your smile
Your laugh
Your love
All joy is absent in this space
Desperately trying not to embrace
The anguish that lingers in the pitch-black sky
My hope has vanished
From my safe place
I've been eternally banished
I fervently question God
Why, oh, why?
Is the moon nowhere in sight?
The clouds unite as your beautiful soul takes flight
The breeze whispers, "Demise"
All signs of life have left your limbs and eyes
In the blink of an eye
Why can't I rewind the time?

CHAPTER 21

Nightmares are Real

C hristopher's entry into the drug scene became full blown and things spiraled out of control quickly. He and his older brother, along with Pam and her friend Cecelia, all got high together on a regular basis. Bandit, the drug dealer, made routine house calls to the home and though he never stayed more than five minutes, he left a lingering impression on Seanette when he smiled and winked at her in a way that made her uneasy.

Pam's and Christopher's weekend ritual was having loud cocaine parties with friends, everyone snorting, freebasing and smoking primos. Pam resorted back to ordering Seanette to stay in her room while they got high all night long. As before in the other apartment, Seanette had to eat and do homework in her room. Though she was curious, she never came out of the room while Pam was entertaining her company. By now, her fearful dread of her mother had returned and she didn't want to get a beating or cussed out.

Usually, the next morning, early in the wee hours, Seanette searched for clues about the night before. She had to know what was going on. Pam and Christopher were very careless about leaving evidence of their cocaine use around the house, which only served to confirm Seanette's suspicions that now they both were addicts. Seanette let her findings percolate in her heart. Instantly, she sank into a deep depression and became flooded with suicidal thoughts. "What would be the least painful way to kill myself?" She asked herself that a lot. She just couldn't understand why she was ever born. She wanted to die. She hated her life and just life, period.

"Seanette, go down to Sunnybrook Farms and buy these groceries," Pam yelled over Cameo's song "Candy" blaring from the stereo. "And don't ride that skateboard." Christopher had given Seanette a skateboard and she couldn't wait to try it out. Pam was in the middle of applying Jheri curl solution to Christopher's hair, so she didn't even notice when Seanette snuck out the door with it. Needless to say, Seanette had gotten about eight blocks when the last of a few daredevil tricks finally took her out and she ended up breaking her leg and dislocating her ankle. A nice old lady immediately called the paramedics and Seanette's mother and stayed right by her side until they came. Although Pam was still processing Christopher's hair, they dropped everything and came to the scene right away. Unfortunately, Christopher's scalp started burning badly and he had to run back to rinse out his hair, but he promised to be at the hospital right after that. And there he was, in the emergency room, right by Seanette's side. She noticed that a lot of his hair had fallen out, which for her was the most selfless act of love any man had done for her.

Seanette's cast went all the way up to her thigh, and she had to wear it for six weeks. The ER doctors said she should be treated and rehabilitated by orthopedic specialists in Los Angeles. Since the school year had just about come to an end when the accident happened and, soon after, Seanette graduated from sixth grade, her mother had her stay with Debbie, Wana and Ty for the first six weeks of summer, since they lived closer to the hospital.

Although Seanette knew everyone in the neighborhood, she really didn't want to be there. Her memories of Debbie's house had made it less inviting, and now that she was there, it was clear that, as time had gone on, the conditions in the home and the neighborhood had gotten worse. And so had Wana and Ty. Debbie was very liberal with her kids. For instance, Seanette was astounded and a little repulsed especially that Wana was getting high and having sex with gang bangers at only eleven years old, two full years younger than her. But Debbie had no rules for Seanette either; the freedom to do whatever she wanted was a treat.

One day, out of the blue, Pam came to take Seanette home. On the way, she announced that she was sending her to her grandmother

Myrtle's house in Cleveland, Ohio, for the last month of summer. Honestly, Seanette wasn't happy or sad about it. She was indifferent because she didn't know anyone in her mother's family out there, so she had no expectations one way or the other.

As they rode to LAX airport, Christopher told Seanette she could call whenever she wanted to, and Pam kept talking about how much fun she was going to have and how many cousins she had. Seanette was just going with the flow. When Seanette arrived in Cleveland, Pam's brother Darrell picked her up and took her to get a bite to eat before heading to Myrtle's house. Myrtle lived in the projects, where she had been for at least twenty years. The environment was not only very different from the San Fernando Valley, it was worse than Debbie's neighborhood in Los Angeles.

Initially, Seanette was excited. Myrtle had custody of several of her grandchildren, so her house was always filled with kids. For Seanette, this meant more cousins to get to know, since Auntie Regina's kids Desi and Angel were the only cousins she was close to. However, that exciting thought was very short-lived. By the close of the first week, she was calling Christopher to see if she could come home. As usual, the music was blaring in the background and she could hardly hear him on the other end. He passed the phone to her mother, who reiterated that Seanette would be staying in Ohio until school started. Before Seanette could ask any other questions, Pam hung up on her. Seanette was devastated. She tried calling back several times, but Pam just let the phone ring.

At first, Seanette's biggest gripe was the living conditions. For one thing, Myrtle kept locks on the deep freezer and the pantry so that no one could access food without her permission. Also, like Pam, Myrtle had a long list of chores for Seanette to do every day, starting with kitchen duty the day she arrived. She also had to clean the living room, mop all the floors, and scrub down all the bathrooms. Worst of all about the living conditions was the roaches. Back home at Pam's, there were "seasonal" roaches mostly in the winter when it was cold, and Pam would spray the apartment down with roach spray and powder. But Myrtle's home was grotesquely infested. There were roaches in the tub. Roaches in the closets. Roaches crawling on the walls. Roaches in the refrigerator. Roaches on the stove. Roaches in the cabinets. Roaches in the washer and dryer. Even roaches outside in the grass. Roaches everywhere in broad daylight and at night. It was disgusting! Seanette hated it!

But soon what she hated the most was how her cousins came to treat her. They had a lot of preconceived biases about her, constantly telling her she thought she was better than them because she lived in California. Seanette was completely confused by this because, sure, she did talk with a different accent, but she didn't act stuck-up. It didn't matter. The more she tried to get along and be like them, the worse they treated her. They even threatened a neighbor's daughter, who was the same age as Seanette, that if she didn't jump Seanette, they would beat her up. Her cousins sat back and laughed as they watched. Seanette counted down the days to leave, because they tormented her the entire time she was there. She was so glad when the summer was over. She never thought she would be so glad to go back to school.

When Seanette finally returned home, things had changed drastically. Pam and Christopher were now fully immersed in their addictions, going from using cocaine just on the weekends to four or five times a week. They had parties throughout the week, and so there were always people at their house. Bandit made routine house calls during the week, as well, and at all times of the night. By the time school started, Seanette's home life was in shambles. As she started seventh grade at North Point, school continued to be a challenge and she fell further and further behind.

It was Saturday, October 3, 1987. Christopher was in the living room assembling a blue beach cruiser for Seanette's 14th birthday, which was still two weeks away. Seanette asked him why he was putting her bike together so far in advance. He said it was just to get it out of the way so she could ride it. Pam, Christopher and Seanette got up early and cleaned the house. It was a beautiful, sunny day, so Christopher decided he wanted to barbeque at the park where he and Pam met. Seanette helped her mother make the potato salad and baked beans, while Christopher seasoned the ribs, hamburger meat and hotlinks.

Then they and Scottie all piled in Christopher's pale blue Monte Carlo, found a great spot and enjoyed a pleasant day.

Near the end of the day, Pam told Seanette to walk Scottie around the park so she and Christopher could spend time alone to talk. Seanette got an attitude and huffed off with Scottie, pouting. During her walk, she fumed outloud to herself about how much she hated them and wanted them to die. Really, she wanted all the attention. She hated her life and wanted to die herself.

Finally, it was time to go home. They first stopped at the local gas station to fill up and got a good laugh as the attendant cracked jokes over the loudspeaker. Next, Pam wanted to stop at a drug dealer's house. Seanette watched intently as her mother got out of the car and knocked on the door. Pam didn't go inside but stood at the stairs and talked with the man briefly. Seanette couldn't tell if they made any exchange. By the time they all arrived home, the sun had set.

After everyone emptied the car, Christopher ate another plate of barbeque while Pam called her friend Lucy. After a few minutes, while her mother was still on the phone in the living room, Seanette met Christopher in the hallway and, with tears in her eyes, told him how sorry she was for the way she acted at the park. He said he understood. Now weeping, Seanette squeezed Christopher with all of her might and said how much she loved him. "Don't cry." He wiped her face with his hand. "I love you, too." "Come on, ya'll!" Pam then yelled from the living room, oblivious to the conversation in the hallway. "Seanette, don't you want to go swimming?"

It seemed a bit abrupt to go to Lucy's house all of a sudden, but Seanette loved to swim. She hurried to her room to put on her bathing suit and then grabbed a towel. During the thirty-minute drive, Christopher had the oldies station on and they all sang along to the radio together. The last song was Ben E. King's "Stand by Me."

Lucy was excited to see everyone, and her two little sons were already in their swimming gear. They lived in a secured apartment complex, so Pam handed Seanette the pool key and told her to take the boys to the pool and watch them there. As Seanette was walking out, she asked Christopher if he was coming. Before he could answer, Pam said, "He'll be out there. Just go to the pool." Seanette really wanted him to come.

She walked out to the pool with Lucy's boys, who were between five and six years younger than her. There were no adults around and no lights, so the pool area was dark. Seanette and the boys jumped in the water and played Marco Polo while they waited for Christopher. After about a half hour had passed, Seanette told the boys to get out of the pool so she could go check on Christopher. She quickly dried off and shuffled to Lucy's apartment. She could hear the music blaring from across the courtyard. She knocked on the door. No answer. She could hear Pam's boisterous voice and laughing coming from inside. She banged and banged on the door some more. When Lucy finally opened it, Seanette saw Christopher and asked him if he was coming out to swim. "In a sec," he replied." Pam told her to go back to the pool and watch the boys, which she did. But she came back three additional times, and each time Pam told her to go back out to the pool.

Back at the pool with the boys, Seanette resigned herself to the conclusion that Christopher wasn't going to join them. So imagine her exuberant shock when she suddenly saw him running at top speed to the pool gate! As soon as she let him in, Christopher immediately dove in. "Marco!" he yelled. "Polo!" Seanette yelled back.

She called it again, "Polo!" And again, "Polo!" Christopher was good at pranking Seanette, so she just assumed he was hiding under the water since it was dark. She called out a couple of times more, "Polo! Polo!" Still no response from Christopher. Now Seanette was frustrated. "Daddy, stop playing!"

It occurred to her in that moment, in that instant, that something was very wrong. She frantically dove under water to find him. She shrieked and cried when she saw his lifeless body face down in the pool. She swam over to him and tried to pull him over to the pool steps. But his body was too heavy to get him all the way there. She felt completely helpless. When she managed to get him to the edge of the steps, his body sank back down to the bottom of the pool. She turned to the boys and told them to go get help. But they were in shock and stood frozen in the pool.

She tried to pull him out of the pool, but to no avail. She couldn't help Christopher. She couldn't save him. She cried out to God. She held and rubbed Christopher's face. "Daddy! Daddy! Please wake up!" Again, no response. She knew she had to leave him to go get help. She got out of the pool and ran to Lucy's front door. The music was still blaring. She banged and banged on the door with a closed fist. No answer. She banged on the door with an open hand. No answer. She sobbed uncontrollably as she prayed and begged for someone to open the door. She had no choice but to wait for the record to go off. What else could she do? How woefully ironic that LTD's "Holding On" was playing.

As soon as the record ended, Seanette resumed banging on the door, yelling for help. Finally, Lucy opened the door. "Help! Come quickly!" Seanette screamed. Pam, noticeably high, drunk and now annoyed, shouted back, "Go back out to the pool! If I have to tell you again, you're getting out." Seanette then cried louder, "My Daddy is dead! Daddy is dead!"

Both Lucy and Pam stood there in a momentary stupor, as if the words had to slowly register before they could move. By now, the boys were at the door crying and wailing, too. Lucy and Pam ran out to the pool. Lucy asked a neighbor to help get Christopher out, while Pam stood and watched from afar. Eventually, paramedics arrived and tried to resuscitate him, continuing their efforts on the way to the hospital. Before heading there themselves, Pam and Seanette drove to Christopher's two older brothers' homes to tell them what happened. They all met up at the hospital and waited for what seemed like an eternity for any updates. When the doctor finally came out of Christopher's room, he let the family know he did not make it. Seanette felt the knot in her stomach quadruple in size. She became completely numb. Pam asked her if she wanted to see Christopher before they took him to the morgue. Seanette was too traumatized already. She had seen and heard enough.

When they returned home, Pam told Seanette to throw away the clothes they had on. And that was it. There was no further processing together how to deal with Christopher's sudden death. Christopher's mother came from Iowa to purchase his funeral clothes and make arrangements for flying his body back home for the services. The entire road trip to Iowa was a blur to Seanette, as was the funeral. In fact, she couldn't even make it all the way through the service because she blacked out, and she didn't go to the cemetery when Christopher was laid to rest. As for Pam, she was high and drunk the entire time. Christopher's death seemed to further propel her into a reckless, downward spiral of addiction.

There is No Title

As I gaze out the window
My mind begins to wander
On a search,
Retrieving memories of both good and bad
Feeling all five senses
Of past times
My soul cringes in pain and laughs in remembrance
As I mentally place myself there
Reliving the experiences over and over
Dodging the impact of the present reality
Praying
Hoping
Maybe it's just a nightmare
Longing to hear the truth
Filled with fear and anger
Deep-rooted sorrow
No hopes for tomorrow
Filled with hate
Choosing food to compensate
My spirit is shattered and scattered
Blowing in the wind

CHAPTER 22
The Sweetest Taboo

P am and Seanette were devastated by Christopher's death, but they didn't talk about it. The subject "Christopher" was pretty much radio silent. There was no processing, no debriefing together. They just went on with their lives, grieving separately and in their own ways. Pam continued to abuse herself with drugs, alcohol and men, and Seanette continued to stuff her emotions with food. Each just had her own unspoken coping mechanism.

A lot did change after Christopher died. One of the biggest changes was that Pam had to enroll Seanette into the local public school since she could no longer afford North Point, although she did allow her to finish out her eighth grade year. The transition to Pete Walters Junior High School (Walters) was tough for Seanette because she did not fit in with any of the kids. Even when she tried to fit in with the black kids, they made fun of the way she talked, dressed and danced. It made her a loner and she felt completely lost. It was interesting, though, that in contrast to her academic struggles at North Point where she was held back a grade, she was placed in honors classes at Walters. That was incomprehensible to Seanette but, nonetheless, she ended up graduating on the Dean's List at the end of the school year of 9th grade.

Unfortunately, even after she turned fifteen, Seanette still wasn't experiencing changes to her body. Besides still struggling to have regular bowel movements, she was still flat chested and still had not started menstruating. She was very ashamed since all the other girls were well progressed in their physical development. She felt no one could relate to her but food. She was almost sixteen when she did finally have her first period. Boy, was she happy! She looked forward every month to getting her period and was very anxious about the rest of her body developing.

Another change after Christopher's death was that Pam started dating again. One night she brought home Charles, who had just gotten out of prison. Frankly, Seanette didn't like him. She did not want to get to know him and had no interest in anything he said. Instead, she withdrew herself further and became more depressed.

Pam started going to Los Angeles again pretty frequently, this time with Charles, and Seanette went with them. Pam and Charles usually dropped Seanette off at Debbie's house before they ventured to wherever, Seanette didn't know or care. The only thing she did know was that they were going to drink and get high. Charles' poisons were gin and PCP. Pam was still abusing cocaine and had returned to occasional PCP.

Seanette started becoming very curious about the street life everyone around her seemed to love so much. Everyone around her glorified sex, drugs, drinking and gang banging. So, she decided to find out first-hand exactly what all the fuss was about.

By now, Debbie's daughter Wana was a full-fledged gang member. Wana had gotten jumped in and had a tattoo representing her loyalty to her gang. She wore her gang colors proudly. She had pretty much stopped going to school and spent all of her time in the 'hood. Now at thirteen years old, she was smoking cigarettes and marijuana, and drinking "forties." She wasn't afraid of anything or anybody, not even death. She carried a gun, sold drugs and had committed crimes that landed her in juvenile hall.

Wana introduced Seanette to the street life and urban culture, including the music. Previously, she listened to Madonna, Wham!, Phil Collins, The Thompson Twins, Huey Lewis and The News, and other pop and alternative bands. She also liked rap and R & B, but fun music like Heavy D & The Boyz, Kid 'n Play, Kwamé, Janet Jackson, Nu Shooz, DeBarge, The Jets and other artists in that vein. However, Wana listened to gangster rappers like N.W.A, DJ Quik, Too Short,

Spice 1, MC Eiht, E-40. She also liked oldies from groups such as The Spinners, The Dells, The Dramatics, The Impressions and The Chi-lites, and slow jam artists like Keith Sweat, Freddie Jackson and Zapp.

Wana took Seanette to 'hood parties and kickbacks, and even to her drug sales. Seanette felt protected when she was around Wana, and Wana still told everyone she was the oldest sister even though she was two years younger. Initially at these gatherings, Wana told everyone Seanette didn't drink or smoke and warned them not to mess with her. Everyone had a lot of respect for Wana because she was down in every sense of the word, that homegirl you called for backup. Point blank! She was there. During these gatherings, Seanette usually sat by herself drinking an orange soda. She quickly grew tired of merely watching everyone else have a good time, feeling like she was on the outside looking in through a window.

One night after a party, Seanette went with Wana and a couple of her friends to a neighborhood school to get high. Seanette stood there awkwardly as Wana and her friends passed a joint around in a circle. Wana's friends started making fun of Seanette, calling her an "L-7." This was a sarcastic term for someone who's being a square. Well, Seanette was sick of being in that box, and she wanted out. So, when they offered her the joint, she grabbed it and took a toke.

This was the second time Seanette had smoked marijuana; she hadn't gotten high since that time with her father a few years back. This time, it was different. She felt the effects immediately. A surge of energy fired off into her brain's neurons and her thoughts and perception were magnified. This caused her to feel a level of relaxation and euphoria she had never experienced before. As her senses dulled, she didn't want to do anything, and she didn't have a care in the world. Unlike that time with Sean when she just got tired and went to sleep, this time, she was relieved of all pain, fear and troubles. No wonder Sean and Pam got high. In that instant moment, she got it, she understood and she felt an overwhelming sense of compassion for them. She couldn't imagine dealing with some of the tragedies that they endured remaining sober.

That high brought about something else in Seanette's thinking. In that moment, in that second, she waivered in her beliefs, goals and dreams. All of a sudden, she felt conflicted about being a virgin until she got married, about never doing drugs, about going off to college and about starting her own family. Now, she wanted to experience instant and tangible gratification. "Why wait on a dream that may not even come true?" she pondered. "This is my new reality, and I need to embrace it. I will be alright. Everyone else is functioning just fine like this, especially Momma."

Seanette was still high when Pam and Charles picked her up from Debbie's house. Thankfully, neither of them noticed; they were in their own world. She just leaned her head back on the seat and fell asleep. She was so glad it happened on a Friday night because she stayed high for at least two more days—plenty of time to sober up before school started on Monday.

Pam and Charles started taking weekend trips away from the house, leaving Seanette at home alone. Seanette began hanging out with some of the neighborhood "cholas," going to all of their weekend kickbacks where these girls would drink beer, snort coke and plot drive-bys and car jackings. All types of people would come through some of these gatherings and she developed a crush on a boy named Pretty Boy, who was in a prominent Mexican gang. Soon, she started hanging out with him and his friends; they would give her rides from school, and she felt so accepted and loved that she started going to ditching parties and kickbacks all the time. Even though she never did coke or drank with them, she did take up smoking cigarettes. Seanette started buying whole packs of cigarettes and kept them in her underwear drawer.

One day, Pam did a surprise search of Seanette's room and found the cigarettes. She had them sitting on the living room table when Seanette came home from school. Pam was very nonchalant when she questioned Seanette about it and even told her to light one up in front of her. Seanette was relieved and lit the cigarette without any hesitation. Pam, however, was mortified when she saw that Seanette actually knew how to inhale. When Seanette finished smoking the cigarette, her mother made her smoke three in a row. Seanette began to feel lightheaded and told her she was okay and didn't want to smoke anymore. Pam became irate and demanded that Seanette eat the cigarettes. Seanette assumed that Pam was joking, but she was quite serious and made her eat several cigarettes until she threw up.

Pam's tactic to stop Seanette from doing what she wasn't supposed to do worked only temporarily. Seanette started secretly acting out in other ways. One night when her mother was gone, Seanette had Pretty Boy and his friends hanging out at her house. At some point they all started teasing her about being a virgin. She tried to deny it, but everyone knew she was lying. Once again, she felt like an outcast. So, when Pretty Boy suggested they play a game of truth or dare, she wanted to play, hoping that someone would dare her to "throw a scam," or make out, with her crush.

Eventually, Pretty Boy dared Seanette to have sex with him. This was more than she bargained for because she was just thinking about making out with him. But she liked that he was showing her some attention. She took Pretty Boy into her bedroom and, just like that, she lost her virginity on a dare. There was nothing special about the act at all, and there was no real emotional connection. They had no relationship. Soon afterwards, Pretty Boy distanced himself from Seanette. He stopped hanging out with her and only paid attention to her when he wanted sex.

As days and weeks passed, Pretty Boy's drug use got worse and he started using crystal meth as well as committing crimes. This led to him going to juvenile hall. It was about this time that Seanette realized her period was late. She sank further into her depression. She wrote him in juvenile hall and told him that she might be pregnant, and then she religiously checked the mailbox every day, but Pretty Boy never replied. Eventually, Seanette's period did come, but she was not relieved; rather, she was more deeply saddened. She had high hopes that if she were carrying his baby, he would love her.

Pretty Boy only spent a few months in jail. He was released on a Friday and Seanette was so happy because it just so happened that Pam and Charles were going away to Las Vegas that same weekend, and she planned to have sex with Pretty Boy while her mother was gone.

She came home from school and cleaned the house up and down as Pam had directed, then she took a shower and patiently waited for Pretty Boy to come by. She waited hours and hours. It was nearly 10:00 when she heard the doorbell ring.

Seanette looked through the peephole and saw a familiar face, but it wasn't Pretty Boy. It was Greg, the boyfriend of one of her friends. Because she knew him, she opened the door without any hesitation. Greg asked if she had seen his girlfriend. When Seanette said no, he asked if he could come in. Seanette didn't consider him a threat at all. She had seen him at a few parties where they exchanged a few cordial words. She invited him in and mentioned that she was waiting for her boyfriend to come by, and he said was going to the store and would keep her company until he did. Seanette saw no problem with that.

When Greg returned, he had a big brown paper bag with two forties and offered one to Seanette. She cracked it open and took a swig, immediately cringing as the sour, bitter, gross liquid infiltrated her body. He encouraged her to sip it down fast, and she did. Again, she wasn't afraid of him. She did not feel she was in imminent danger even though they were alone.

By now, Seanette was feeling the effects of the beer. She was sweating, her speech was slurred, she was losing control of her mental faculties, and her equilibrium was off. Greg asked if he could use the bathroom. When he returned, he was naked. Seanette asked him to put his clothes back on, but he refused. He grabbed her wrist and pulled her towards the couch. She tried to pull away from him, but he was strong and threw her on the couch. She continued to struggle as he yanked off her clothes. Seanette closed her eyes and imagined her safe place. She felt the butterflies covering her and hovering over her body as Greg raped her.

Seanette must have passed out during the incident but woke up in the middle of the night nauseated. All the lights in the living room were still on, but Greg was gone. She ran to the bathroom and threw up, and then she cried and threw up some more. She took the clothes she had been wearing and threw them in the trash, and then drew herself a bath. She made the water steaming hot and sat in it until it turned cold. Then she rocked herself to sleep as she cried.

Pam and Charles returned Sunday afternoon. Seanette never spoke about what happened. She stuffed it into the pit of her stomach, on top of all the other painful and traumatic experiences she had been through. Seanette was sixteen years old.

If It Isn't Love

The sound of your voice so hypotonic
Mesmerized by your conversation
Your smile gentle as your touch
Is this teenage love?
Whatever this is
I don't ever want it to end
You cast a spell on me
I can't eat
Sleep
Think
About anything else but you
I am infatuated with everything about you
You have taken over my dreams
My reality
I fantasize of being with you all the time
I live and breathe for the next moment with you
For without you
I have no will
No purpose to live

CHAPTER 23

Love Jones

Seanette's self-esteem plummeted after the rape. She could not erase the images from her head. She felt so dirty and disgusted with herself, taking excessive showers to wash off all the dirt and shame. She blamed herself. She felt stupid. She caused this. It was her fault. She continued to stuff her feelings with food and contemplated suicide frequently. Although she attended school regularly, she didn't try very hard; mentally she had checked out and her grades suffered. She'd sit in class and daydream of being alone in the fields with her butterfly friends. She still didn't have any real friends to confide in, only acquaintances, and she usually ate alone. She was glad Christmas break was coming. She knew she would have an outlet at Debbie's house.

Pam agreed to let Seanette stay at Debbie's house over Christmas break. She even gave Seanette her Christmas presents early: a pair of blue-and-white tennis shoes, a blue-and-white windbreaker, and two pairs of corduroys with shirts to match. Pam got everything she asked for, but little did she know Seanette was slowly associating herself with the gang culture.

It was a Friday afternoon when Pam and Seanette pulled up to Debbie's house. Her mother gave her fifty dollars and told her not to spend it all in one place. Every kid in the neighborhood was outside laughing and playing. The older homeboys were racing their cars down the street, flossing their hydraulics while blasting their music. The day was perfect! Seanette was right where she wanted to be. Free! She was going to make the most of Debbie's lax rules.

Seanette thanked her mother for the money, jumped out of the car and ran into the house. Wana was taking a bath, getting ready for the night out. She told Seanette about a kickback in the 'hood later. Seanette was so excited; she kept pestering Wana to hurry up so she could take a bath. Wana just laughed and continued to swish the water around in the tub.

When Wana finally came out of bathroom, Seanette jumped in, out and into her clothes in no time. Then, once night fell, Seanette and Wana bailed to the 'hood. The streets were flooded with the homies and neighbors from the 'hood, so as Seanette and Wana strolled along, they stopped periodically to chat briefly with the homies standing on their porches. When they arrived at the party, Seanette was thrilled. She and Wana greeted everyone with dap and a "What's up." Wana immediately grabbed a forty, but Seanette was cool on the alcohol. The last time she had a forty, she ended up getting raped. The party was in someone's backyard, with a DJ and strobe lights, and it was packed. Seanette stood on the concrete wall by herself and vibed off of "Atomic Dog" by George Clinton. She took a sip of her soda and lit a cigarette.

"You know you' too pretty to be smoking cigarettes. You don't even look right smoking." Seanette didn't notice him creep up behind her. She rolled her eyes and thought to herself, "What nerve this dude has. He's smoking himself." Still, there was something very mysterious about this guy. She didn't even know his name, but she was drawn to him. His skin was smooth and silky, like dark chocolate. He was slim and well over six feet tall. His teeth were creamy and white as whole milk. He had an infectious laugh. He didn't seem to have a care in the world.

The DJ changed the song to "I Wanna Be Your Man" by Zapp & Roger. Seanette was so nervous. She had never danced with a boy before and was afraid of what was going to happen next. Feelings of abandonment and rejection rose up in her head, but before the feelings overtook her entire being, he gently grabbed her hand and led her to the middle of the crowd on the dance floor. Seanette took a deep breath and savored the moment. He held on to the small of her back and slowly rocked her back and forth to the rhythm of the music. He was a gentleman. He didn't try to take advantage, and he was polite. "Who is this guy?" she thought to herself. "Where did he come from, and why did he choose me?" When the song was over, he whispered four words in her ear, "I'll see you around." Then he disappeared in the crowd. That was it. She didn't even catch his name or exchange phone numbers.

Shortly after that, Wana and Seanette caught a ride home with one of the homies. Seanette could not stop thinking about that guy. She didn't even want to take a shower. She wanted the smell of his cologne to stay on her body and clothes forever. She dreamt of this mystery guy and replayed the whole night in her mind over and over.

The next day was filled with as much adventure as the night before. There was another party in the 'hood and Seanette was so giddy about the prospect of seeing the mystery guy again, she couldn't wait!

Finally, nighttime came. Seanette and Wana got dressed and headed out. At the party, Seanette scanned the crowd for the mystery guy, but he wasn't there. Her spirits dropped. Wana was having such a good time drinking, smoking marijuana, dancing with the homies and socializing with everyone, she never noticed Seanette sitting alone on the porch, uninterested. A few guys tried to talk to her, but she ignored them or only partly listened to their conversation.

Seanette and Wana were among the last few people to leave. Wana told Seanette "the homeboy" was going to take them home. That's when Seanette noticed the white Cadillac with twenty-inch, blue Dayton wire rims pull up to the curb. Low and behold, the mystery guy was in the driver's seat! Seanette's heart leaped in her chest. She got in the backseat along with one of the guys who had been trying to talk to her all night. She hoped the mystery guy didn't think this was her boyfriend. Wana got in the front seat and they drove around the 'hood. The mystery guy lit a joint and passed it to Wana. While the two of them laughed and chatted, the guy sitting with Seanette tried to pick up on Seanette. His name was Blaze, from the 'hood. He bragged about the fact that he was "courted on" by the big homies, acting like

Seanette should be impressed that he was allowed into the gang verbally, without having to be jumped in, probably because he knew someone or had a relative or big homie from the same set.

Seanette couldn't care less what Blaze was talking about. It was the mystery guy who intrigued her and had her attention. But she never got a chance to talk with him that night. This, of course, only fed her curiosity. The mystery guy dropped her and Wana off at Debbie's house and drove off—but she still didn't get his name! Maybe he really was a mystery guy. She didn't say anything to Wana, though. She just kept her feelings to herself.

But the next day, she woke up even more frustrated! "Why won't he tell me his name?" Without bothering to get herself together once she was up, she joined Wana on the porch with the rest of the homies. Then she saw him! The mystery guy was right at the house across the street, washing his car in the driveway! Seanette could not believe the mystery guy was living right there this whole time! Her heart fluttered.

She mustered up the nerve to ask Wana who the mystery guy was. But before she could, he started strolling across the street towards them. Seanette noticed how his walk was proud and confident. "Who is that?" she quickly whispered to Wana. "Oh, that's the homeboy Dom," Wana replied. "Dom?" "Oh, his real name is Dominic, but everybody calls him Dom." Dom walked right up to the porch and introduced himself to Seanette. "What up, I'm Dom. What's yo' name?" Wana interjected, "This is my little sister Seanette. She from the Valley." He told Seanette to come over after she took a bath.

Seanette was so embarrassed. Was it that noticeable that she had just jumped out of bed and came right outside? She immediately went to the bathroom and took a look at herself in the mirror. Total bed head! She bathed, got dressed for the day and was finishing up her hair when Wana asked her, "You like Dom, huh?" Seanette didn't quite know how to answer her. First of all, she didn't even know him, and second, she really didn't want anyone knowing. After all, she didn't want to be rejected and embarrassed if by some chance he had a girlfriend. As she contemplated on exactly what to say, she simply responded with a smile. A huge smile. She realized he was an active gangbanger, but she was completely enamored with him. She just wanted to be around him and get to know him. He seemed so mature.

Dom was finishing up washing his car when Seanette crossed the street and walked towards him. Dom had X Clan's "Funkin' Lesson" blasting from his speakers. She was very impressed with his EQ system which included speakers in the car and in the trunk, something she had never seen before. She also admired his muscles and tattoos as he waxed his tires, something she noticed when she approached his car.

At first, Dom didn't seem to notice Seanette standing there. He was in his own world as he bobbed his head to the music. Growing impatient, she stood there awkwardly for a moment, trying to figure out a way to get his attention. She knew she would be in competition with the music since he had it up so loud, so she leaned on the side of the car. He had to notice her then. It worked, alright. Dom gave her a bright smile. "Oh, so you think you special that you can just lean on my car?" Seanette couldn't contain her emotions. She smiled wide back at him, they both laughed and the conversation flowed from there. Dom told Seanette he was originally from Chicago but came out west to visit his family. Seanette didn't ask any questions. She just listened intently to every word he said. Not that he said much, but she was just glad to have his attention.

Dom gave Seanette a dozen compliments about her hair and complexion. This was the first time a guy had ever paid her a compliment. He told her she should be proud of her hair and complexion. He also told her how smart she was and that one day, she was going to go to college and be somebody. Seanette grew tired of this part of the conversation. She had heard this "go to school" bit all before from everyone her entire life. She rolled her eyes, opened the passenger car door and slid in. Dom caught the door and shut it for her. Seanette was over the moon with him. What a gentleman he was.

Dom then got in the car and grabbed a pack of cigarettes from above the visor to have a smoke. Seanette took out a cigarette for herself, lit it and took a drag. Dom looked confused as he watched her. "Didn't I tell you the other night you don't even look right smoking?" He grabbed her cigarette and threw it out the window. "Why did you do that?" she asked, a little annoyed. "I told you. You don't belong here. You need to be thinking about going to college. This is not the life you want." Seanette suddenly felt stupid. She didn't know how to respond. She didn't have a comeback. She just sat in the car and stared out the window.

Dom changed the subject, "Hey, you wanna go to the movies tonight?" "Oh, wow. Did he just ask me out on a date?" Seanette thought to herself. "Quick, dummy, hurry up and answer." She replied, "Sure, that's cool." "Okay, meet me here at my house tonight around seven-thirty. I got some business to take care of before that." "Wow," she thought, "Business? He must be important."

Seven-thirty couldn't come fast enough. Seanette asked Debbie if she could go, and of course, Debbie said yes. She didn't even give her a curfew. All this made Seanette feel grown. She changed her clothes three times before she settled on the "right" outfit. Wana joked with her about finally losing her virginity. No one knew that she lost her virginity to Pretty Boy or about the rape by Greg. Those were experiences she planned to take to the grave.

Just as promised, Dom was waiting at seven-thirty. Seanette was so nervous. She had never been on a real date and in fact had never felt wanted by a boy, so she was completely taken back by his genuine interest in her. He took her to the drive-in where they saw a double feature, "Child's Play" and "Kindergarten Cop." Dom held her hand throughout both movies and even offered to buy some popcorn. Seanette was in heaven. This must be love! This is it! All that she had been searching for was right in front of her. Dom was a perfect gentleman on that date. He didn't try to force himself on her at all. At the end of the night, he reached over, gently brushed the side of Seanette's face, and kissed her. Passionately. She had never French-kissed anyone before, but Dom was an expert. She could've sworn she saw stars. As they sat in the car and listened to the radio for a while, Michel'le's "Something in My Heart" came on. Seanette listened closely to every word. It was a sure sign to hear such a beautiful song after such a perfect night, and it became their song.

Every day after that until the weekend before school started, Dom and Seanette were together. He even asked her to be his girlfriend.

Then her mother found out. Pam had called one night and Debbie told her Seanette was out with her boyfriend. She was not liking this at all, questioning Debbie about who Dom was, how long they had been gone and when they were returning. Debbie offered no answers except to say, "Pam, I don't know, but the girl is sixteen years old." The next day, Pam arrived bright and early to pick Seanette up. Seanette was so glad Dom wasn't around, but her mother assured her she would bring her back the next weekend or so just so she could meet him.

Seanette was so sad when she had to return to school. She had to get back to Los Angeles before the next school break, which wouldn't be until Presidents' Day or maybe Easter break.

When It All Falls Down

Broken dreams and promises
You left inside my heart
Chronicles of teenage love
I didn't have a clue
Living in a bubble
Of made up storybook romance and fairy tales
Trying to escape from my reality
This recurring pain
So deep
So high
So wide
It drives
Me
It taunts
Me
I want to die

CHAPTER 24
Love Rollercoaster

Seanette forgot all about her report card and her grades for the first semester of tenth grade. She had left school worries behind over the Christmas break. Well, her mother sure didn't forget and had the report card sitting on the coffee table when they got home from Los Angeles. "Can you explain to me why you got a D- in math and a D in earth science?" It was a rhetorical question.

Before Seanette could reply, Pam quickly got up and went to her room. Seanette picked up her report card. She got an A in English, a B in psychology, an A in drama and a C in P.E., besides the two Ds. She was puzzled. Why did her mother fail to mention the other grades and just zero in on the two Ds? Seanette began to cry. She knew why she got those bad grades. It wasn't for lack of trying hard; she just didn't understand math or science.

Pam returned with an extension cord and demanded that Seanette take her clothes off. Seanette tried to plead with her, but to no avail. Pam began to strike her all over her body with the cord and wouldn't stop in spite of Seanette's yelps and wails. When she was done, she told her stay in her room for the rest of the day. Seanette looked at her skin. She had deep purple welts and bruises all over her arms, legs, back, chest and bottom. Her mother left for the rest of the day but told Seanette to clean up the entire house while she was gone.

Seanette was so embarrassed by her wounds. She prayed the bruises would be gone by Monday when she went to school. Sunday came and went, but the bruises had only grown worse. The skin on some of them was opened and had bled when she took a shower. That Monday, she covered up the bruises by wearing Christopher's old grey jacket. It was a hot Monday morning as she walked to school and thought about how she could get out of her mother's house.

She was too afraid to run away. She didn't know where she could go or what she would have to do. She was scared to tell anyone in her family about the beatings, given how it backfired when she told her cousin Angel. Then it came to her—a solution that wouldn't hurt anyone and she wouldn't have to answer to anyone. She could just disappear. When she arrived at school, her mind raced with all the possible scenarios of committing suicide.

Seanette had first period English, homeroom and second period drama in the same second-floor room with Ms. Wilson. Ms. Wilson was her favorite teacher. She was so compassionate and easy to talk to, and she truly loved her job. During first and second period, Seanette just stared out the window thinking about jumping, but it had security bars. She became more despondent as she began to feel there was no way out. She felt trapped. By the end of second period, she was a mess inside, completely distraught and inconsolable. She walked up to Ms. Wilson and started to cry. Ms. Wilson grabbed a chair and Seanette told her what her mother had done, showing her teacher the marks on her body. Ms. Wilson held Seanette's hand and listened intently as she spoke.

Ms. Wilson informed Seanette that as a teacher, she was required to report the abuse. Seanette began to cry again and begged her not to tell. Ms. Wilson told Seanette that part of her job was to protect kids. Then she sent her down to the nurse's office.

The nurse seemed annoyed at first. She showed no compassion nor was she discreet, asking Seanette to show her the marks and bruises in the open area instead of privately. Embarrassed and ashamed, Seanette took off Christopher's jacket and the nurse gasped and then offered her a seat. The nurse took pictures of Seanette's arms, chest and legs. She then asked if there were any other areas with bruises and Seanette told her on her back and bottom. The nurse had Seanette lift her shirt up, and she photographed her back. Seanette was then excused to go to class. The rest of the day at school went like a blur. Seanette was petrified to go home. She didn't know what to expect.

When she got home, her mother was already there, and the house was spotless. At first, Pam was very distant and had few words to say to Seanette, but Seanette assumed the school had called because of her mother's attitude and body language. But before Seanette could draw too many conclusions on her own, Pam finally spoke.

"So, the school called me today," she started. Then the rapid fire questions and ranting began. "Who were you talking to? You don't like living here? What lies did you tell on me? If you don't like it here, then leave. You have them calling me on my job? You are ungrateful. You called them just because I smoke weed. So what? It's only weed. Don't I give you a good life? I have sacrificed so much for you. You are so ungrateful. You can leave today. You trying to hurt me? I don't care what you told them. You are going to tell them everything is okay here in my house. Don't go running your mouth telling nobody what goes on in my house. This is my house, do you understand? I am going to leave my weed box right here under the glass table. I dare you to say something. You got the problem. I am not the one with the problem. I should whoop you again. Oh, so you afraid of me? We goin' sit here and wait for the social worker together." Seanette never got the opportunity to answer because on and on her mother went.

The social worker, a thin elderly white lady, arrived at five o'clock that evening. Pam offered her a seat on the couch, saying, "Come in. I don't have nothing to hide." The social worker asked a few basic, preliminary questions, but when it came time to discuss the physical abuse incident, she interviewed Seanette in front of Pam. First, the social worker asked Pam about the incident as well as her drug use. Pam denied any drug abuse and minimized the physical abuse. The social worker then turned to Seanette and repeated the same questions to her that she just asked Pam. What was Seanette to do? She lied and said they didn't happen. At that, the social worker thanked Pam for her time and left. She didn't even leave a business card.

Get your stuff and get out of my house," demanded Pam as soon as the lady left. Pam called Diane and told her that Seanette was messing up in school and was rebellious. She then had Seanette pack all of her things, took her to Diane's house and sped off. Diane made it very clear to Seanette that she could stay a couple of days, but she had to work it out with her mother. After two days, Seanette was back at home. Her mother seemed more annoyed and angry, but there was no discussion about what happened. They just went on, as usual.

Seanette lived for the weekends. It was time she cherished because she got to be with Dom. The more time they spent together, the deeper she fell in "love" with him, even without sex. He had become her primary focus, her sole reason for living. She didn't talk or think about anything else. Dom was her world. She dreamed about him. She wrote poems about him. She put pictures of him in her school folder. She cried at night, every night that she wasn't with him. She was completely obsessed with him, and everybody knew it. Dom knew it, Wana knew it and all the homies knew it, too. In fact, they teased her about it and she had to laugh along with them because she knew it was true. But she didn't care.

One Friday when Pam dropped Seanette off at Debbie's house, the street was unusually quiet. This was strange. Typically, everyone would be outside playing music, dancing, talking and just kicking it. Seanette looked across the street and Dom's car was not parked in his parents' driveway. At first, she didn't think anything of it. He probably went to the store or to "handle some business" like he always spoke of. She went into the house and watched cartoons with Debbie's son Ty until Wana came home.

That's when the bomb dropped. Wana had come home to bathe and then head out again. Seanette asked her about Dom and Wana told her, "Yea, I seen him. He had to go back to Chicago," Wana began to tell her. "You know he sell dope. Girl, he got a girl, a baby and another one on the way."

Seanette couldn't believe it! No! She had no idea. No one had told her. Wana kept talking, but Seanette had already tuned her out. How come nobody told her? She was hurt and furious.

That was the longest weekend ever! To her own surprise, Seanette actually wanted to go home. She almost literally jumped into the car when her mother came to pick her up on Sunday afternoon. She was in a daze. A fog. She cried for weeks. She barely passed tenth grade and had to go to summer school to make up her grades. She didn't return to Los Angeles until Christmas break.

Out of Place

Out of place
Occupying space
Trying to keep a smile on my face
Desperate to fit in
Anywhere
Fighting to hold back these tears
Watching
Waiting
Hoping
Holding on
To nothing but years
And dated memories
I struggle with what to think or even say
This pain
I wish and pray it away
It is constant
Ever-present
Always near
Throbbing
Loud
You are just like everyone
You claimed to be different
But you were like them
Exactly the same
I want to get off this ride
I do not want to play your game

CHAPTER 25
The Naked Truth

When Seanette returned to Los Angeles for Christmas break, a lot had changed and she stayed only for a few days. Dom went to jail for selling drugs, Wana went to juvenile hall for aggravated assault, and Ty got jumped into the gang, started smoking weed and began jacking car stereos out of neighbors' cars. This left Seanette without anyone to hang with, so she stayed only a few days and spent some time with Dom's younger stepsister Danielle. Thankfully, they had a lot in common. Danielle also went to an all-white school in the Valley (she was bussed there), and she liked the same music and fashion. Plus, she kept it real.

She gave Seanette the lowdown on Dom and kept apologizing for how things turned out with him. She told her that Dom was only one year older than Seanette, but he had lived a fast, hard life that made him grow up very quickly because his mother was on drugs, which left him to help take care of his siblings. Dom met and fell in love with Justine when they were twelve years old, and they started having children early. This was the reason why Dom came to California and moved in with them, so that his dad could help him find a better way to live to take care of his kids than selling drugs and gangbanging. Justine stayed behind in Chicago with the children and was waiting for him to return, but when he got back, he got caught selling drugs and went to jail. He was planning to return to California with her and their kids when he got out.

That was the story in a nutshell. Seanette was blown away. She felt so many emotions. On the one hand, she was sad for Dom and Justine, that they had such "grownup problems" so early in their lives. But she was also mad at him for not telling her the truth. On top of that, she was jealous of Justine that she had a family of her own. And she was miserable that Dom was away. It would be a long time before she would hear anything from him. She felt alone, confused, anxious and dejected.

All of this only helped to plunge Seanette deeper into her despondency. She was stripped of any desire to do anything, and she just stopped caring. She continued going to school and finished up eleventh grade, but her self-care severely suffered.

To make matters worse, problems between her mother and Charles had escalated. He was back and forth to jail, and when he was out, he and Pam would argue and he physically and verbally abused her in front of Seanette. He would also break things in the house. Then he'd take off for weeks in her car.

The house was always so peaceful when Charles wasn't there. Pam was still using and, in fact, the extra stress of their volatile interaction temporarily elevated her drug use. But he always came back, and never had to explain where he had been. He just reappeared after weeks, sometimes months, and every time, Pam welcomed him with open arms. When he did return, he always appeared to be under the influence, and he always brought people with him, like his brothers or cousins to "spend a spell." Then he'd always complain about how tired he was from being out in the streets and how there was never any food in the house.

The lack of food in the house was still a constant problem, and Pam still coerced Seanette to call Diane when it was time to ask for help. Like always, Diane questioned what foods they had, what they didn't have, and why they didn't have it. Seanette became an expert at not being defensive or confrontational. She just went with the flow and accepted everything anyone said about her or her mother, whether good or bad.

This attitude and behavior really came from the fact that Seanette had no ambition, no goals and no dreams. Instead, she envisioned daily how to end her life, and every day she prayed to die. She hated her life, she hated herself and she didn't believe in anything or anyone except all the negative thoughts that bombarded her mind constantly. She felt her home life was in shambles and saw no way out. And now that all of her plans to have Dom go with her to all of her senior year activities was no longer an option, what was there left in life to look forward to? "If only I could talk to Dom."

Then, Seanette came up with the bright idea to write him in jail. After all, she knew his first, middle and last names, plus his birth date. So, she called the county jail in Chicago and the officer she spoke to confirmed Dom was there and gave her a physical address where she could send letters to him. She wrote him and eagerly waited for him to send a reply. To her pleasant surprise, he not only wrote her back but also promised to come see her when he got out.

That helped ease Seanette's depression, but not enough to erase her suicidal thoughts. She still sought out a plan to kill herself, thinking long and hard about the least painful method. She frequently spent the weekends at Diane's house and so, during one visit; she got the idea to take a few of Otis' pills. Otis was now on several medications following a couple of heart attacks, a stroke that left one side of his body partially paralyzed, and a triple bypass. Seanette didn't look at the bottles; she just took a few pills out of each one and stuffed them in her pocket.

When Diane dropped her off at home, Seanette hid the pills in an old Tylenol bottle in her medicine cabinet. She decided she would take the pills over the next weekend and anxiously trudged through that whole week of school. When the weekend came, Seanette began to carry out her suicide plan. First, she wrote one last entry in her journal, and then took the pills out of the bottle. Next, she played three songs in order on her stereo: "Crazy for You" by Madonna in remembrance of Robert, "Angel Baby" in remembrance of Pretty Boy, and "Something in My Heart" by Michel'le in remembrance of Dom. She then went to have one last conversation with her momma.

As Seanette entered her mother's room, Pam was on the bed watching TV. Seanette began to cry and told her she was very sad, wanted to kill herself and already had a plan. To Seanette, her mother showed only minimal concern. Pam asked her how she planned to kill herself.

Seanette showed her the pills and told her where she got them from. Pam then opened her nightstand drawer, took out the phone directory and handed it to Seanette. "Since you want to kill yourself," she said to her daughter, "look in this book and find you some help." Not knowing how to respond and especially where to look, Seanette took the phone-book and self-consciously flipped through the pages. Sitting with her mother, she felt completely helpless.

"You do know that if you kill yourself, you are going to hell," Pam went on to say. "That's a sin." Seanette left her mother's room with those words reverberating through her heart, mind and soul. "If you kill yourself, you are going to hell." She wasn't sure that was in the Bible — she had never seen it. But she definitely did not want to go to hell.

Seanette was afraid of God and didn't want to disappoint Him, but she was very confused about her life and why He allowed so many awful things to happen to her. She was afraid to ask Him out loud in prayer, but she really wanted to understand. So she started writing Him letters, starting each one with the salutation, "Dear Father God."

Seanette found comfort in these letters and soon was writing to God all the time. She found a sense of solace in writing down her thoughts and prayers.

Running on Empty

Running thoughts of suicide
Infiltrate my mind
No peace to find
Clouding my judgment
Searching for love
I am surrounded by total darkness and despair
I have not a single care
My hope is gone
My faith is diminished
Oh God
Give me the courage to finish
I am restless
I am worthless
I do not eat or sleep
My actions are careless
No motivation
To think about anything
Only death

CHAPTER 26

If You Can't Beat 'Em, Join 'Em

Seanette managed to pass the first semester of twelfth grade by the skin of her teeth, but there was still a pressing issue looming over her head for graduation. She still could not pass the math portion of the High School Competency Exam (HSCE), which she had been taking and failing since the tenth grade. Pam talked about it every day, never asking why Seanette had such a hard time with it but just constantly threatening, "You better pass that test."

Seanette didn't know what to do. She felt worthless and stupid. She tried to push it out of her mind, but it always crept back up, especially whenever someone at school talked about prom and all the other special senior class events. She was even more depressed talking about the prom, because she had planned to go with Dom.

Then she got some good news. She had been in contact with Dom's stepsister Danielle, who said he was coming back to L.A. around Christmas. Seanette was so excited, and Pam agreed to allow her to spend the Christmas break at Debbie's house.

As usual, Pam dropped Seanette off on a Friday and, as usual, everyone was outside just hanging out and playing music. Debbie, Wana and Ty were home this time, and Wana was already dressed and ready to head out. She was going to the nail shop. Pam had given Seanette two hundred dollars for Christmas, so she had already planned to get her nails done and her hair braided, and to go shopping.

Wana and Seanette took the bus straight to the swap meet. They got long acrylic nails with blue polish and the pinky nail painted gold.

Seanette also got a gold initial "D"—for Dom—put on her ring finger. They bought matching outfits, boots and the items required for braiding, including blue rubber bands. Seanette couldn't wait to get dookie braids. Everyone was wearing them, even all the singers and groups and their video dancers, from Janet Jackson to Soul II Soul. Wana had a homegirl who braided and offered to do their hair for twenty-five dollars each.

For their last stop, they headed downtown to the Alley to buy some gold jewelry. Seanette loved shopping with Wana because she knew where to go for all the deals and the latest fashions. Seanette purchased eight rings (one for almost every finger) and two pairs of gold bamboo earrings. She was ready, and she still had money left over. It was a long Friday, but the night was young and she and Wana were ready to party.

Seanette and Wana walked to the 'hood in their new outfits, shoes, gold jewelry and blue rubber bands at the ends of their fresh dookie braids. Wana rolled a blunt while they walked, lit it, took a couple of tokes and passed it to Seanette. With no hesitation, Seanette hit the blunt a few times. She wanted to relieve herself from the world, the HSCE, Dom and Justine, her mother, the depression, the anxiety, the fear, the worthlessness, the low self-esteem, the self-hatred and the loneliness. She wanted to escape. She wanted all the pain and trauma to leave her entire being—her mind, body and soul. She didn't think about the consequences. She only thought about right now. And right about now, she was feeling darn good.

While they walked, Wana clowned Seanette about Dom. Seanette laughed it off but then declared her love for Dom. Wana sang parts of "Something in My Heart" to playfully mock Seanette. "Girl, you are so sprung on him," she said. "I can't believe you didn't have sex with him. That's too deep for me. What's up with that?" Seanette just smiled and said, "Yeah, that's 'cause what we have is real." She was so gullible. The truth was, Dom had her mind, which made her far more vulnerable than sex would have. He could've have told her to jump off a building, and she would've done it.

Seanette and Wana continued to walk the dark streets on the east side without a care in the world, chatting, laughing and clowning on one another. As they approached a series of abandoned buildings along the block, a strange voice came from above their heads. "What up, blood?" They both looked up and saw a young guy dressed in all red, pointing a sawed-off shotgun at them. They replied in unison with a "What's up" and a head nod. The young guy then said, "Ya'll be safe." They replied in unison again, "Right, right." Wana didn't seem scared, but Seanette was shaken. It was cool to associate with the gangbangers, but getting "banged on" or "hit up" like that was something else entirely. Thankfully, they arrived to the 'hood safely.

Seanette's high was blown after that experience, so she definitely wanted to get high again. And not just high but high as a kite. The homies had plenty of forties and all kinds of alcohol, weed and anything else you could want in the 'hood. Seanette still avoided alcohol, but she was becoming a regular marijuana smoker, or "budhead," and she still smoked cigarettes.

After awhile, Seanette noticed from afar Wana talking about what had transpired earlier. She was laughing and smiling like it was normal. It dawned on Seanette that getting hit up was normal in the 'hood. This entire scene was very ordinary for Wana and the homies. She stood there admiring all the camaraderie around her. She always felt safe in Wana's 'hood. She knew that if anything happened, everybody would protect one another. Everyone had each other's back, like true sisters and brothers. She had witnessed it time and time again. As DJ Quik's "Tonite" blared from one of the homie's cars and a blunt was passed to her, Seanette inhaled not only the blunt but the atmosphere, too.

Seanette wanted to belong. She wanted to be a part of this kinship. She even reflected on how things might have been different for her if one of the homies knew about Greg, her rapist. They probably would have put their hands on him and hurt him in the worst way. She felt better about herself just being around them. She didn't have any issues with her self-esteem or her perception of herself. She felt free!

"Get down! Everybody, get down!" Seanette's thoughts were abruptly interrupted by the urgent shouts of one of the big homies. Then came the sound of gunshots and screeching tires. The homies all ran towards the street corner with guns drawn, while Seanette knelt down next to a nearby car for safety. Wana ran to her side, quickly checked on her, and then joined the homies with her gun drawn, too. Curiously, Seanette wasn't even worried. She was proud to be able to say she experienced both being "banged on" and a drive-by all in one night. "Wow! This vacation is off to a good start," she thought to herself.

Fortunately, after it was all over, no one got hurt and they all laughed about it as they resumed their drinking and getting high.

It was about two o'clock in the morning when the kickback died down and one of the big homies offered Seanette and Wana a ride home. They first stopped at the neighborhood burger spot where the girls shared some chili cheese fries and drank strawberry sodas. By the time they finally got to Debbie's house, it was close to three o'clock in the morning. Wana and Seanette didn't wake up until about noon the next day, and when they did, they went on the porch, smoked cigarettes and kicked it with the homies.

Seanette didn't really want to have a conversation with anyone but Dom. Her being outside was just an excuse to spy on him, but he still wasn't there. Her nerves were in knots. She prayed and even wished on a star that he would show up. She missed him so much. She loved him and actually thought about having sex with him. "Maybe that's why he keeps having children with Justine," she thought. By now, they had another baby and Justine was pregnant with their fourth. This made three boys, all named with the letter "D" after their daddy. But she didn't care if Dom had a football team with Justine. She was just so sprung on him and wanted to be with him any way or any how possible.

As the next few days passed, Seanette sulked around Debbie's house as she waited for Dom's return, refusing to go anywhere. She didn't want to go to the 'hood or any kickbacks or parties. Then, on the day before the last day of Christmas break, Wana was finally able to persuade her to go to a kickback. Actually, she didn't have to try too hard because Seanette was depressed and wanted an escape.

Seanette did not put that much effort into getting dressed up. Since Dom wasn't around, she didn't have anyone to impress and didn't want to talk to anyone but him. She slicked her hair back in a ponytail with some gel and threw on some jean shorts, a t-shirt, scrunch socks, her blue and white tennis shoes, her ski sport blue-and-white jacket, her blue-faced watch, and her portable cassette player. It was the latest edition and had a built-in equalizer and auto-reverse.

As she and Wana walked to the party, she popped Rob Base's and DJ E-Z Rock's "It Takes Two" tape into her cassette player and cranked it up on full volume. Seanette was so engrossed and rapping along with the music that she wasn't paying attention to where they were going. When they hit a corner she wasn't familiar with, she asked Wana where they were going. "Oh, the homie Lil' Insane is having a kickback," replied Wana. Seanette really didn't care for Lil' Insane. He was very violent and beat up all of his girlfriends to the point where they were unrecognizable. He was impulsive and explosive, and he was constantly in and out of jail.

As soon as they arrived, Seanette sensed this was a bad idea. She felt completely uncomfortable and out of place. Wana could tell she didn't want to be there, so she tried to reassure her by saying they weren't going to stay long. Blaze, the guy who tried to talk to her in the car the second time she ever saw Dom, walked up to her and sparked up a conversation. Seanette felt semi-safe with him because at least she had met him before, but still, she didn't really know him that much.

Wana approached them and asked Seanette, "You straight?" Seanette nodded, and Wana passed her the blunt. Seanette closed her eyes and inhaled two long tokes. She just wanted to disappear, to relieve her mind of all mental and emotional distress. Life was just so overwhelming for her. She felt like she was on a merry-go-round and she wanted it to stop. She wanted to get off this ride. She felt trapped and, for now, her only escape was to numb her pain.

While Seanette and Blaze talked, Lil' Insane yelled out, "Aye, come here, let me holla at you." Seanette wasn't sure who he was talking to, and since she had never had a conversation with him, she assumed he was talking to someone else. He trotted over to where she, Wana and Blaze were standing. "Hey, you think you too good to talk to me?" he said to Seanette. "I told you to come here." Before she could respond, he started shouting profanities and obscenities towards her, and then he roughly grabbed her wrist and snatched her close to him. Seanette just stood there in shock as he slapped her face. "'Nette, run!" Wana yelled.

Seanette yanked back her wrist and ran. She heard Blaze behind her, "No, this way." He was running, too, to make sure she was okay. Seanette didn't know who to trust, but since she was in a different 'hood, she followed his lead. Her heart was beating so fast as they ran in the dark through the streets. Blaze led her to the back gate of a middle school. Of course, the gate was locked, and it was at least fifteen feet high. "Come on and climb the gate," he told her. Seanette watched him climb to the top effortlessly and then launch himself into a back flip and land on the concrete on the other side.

She was amazed and scared all at the same time. Blaze called out to her, "Don't be afraid. I will catch you. You won't fall." Seanette slowly climbed the gate, but when she got to the top, she froze in fear and just straddled the fence. Deathly afraid of heights, she looked down at the ground and began to panic. "Don't look down. Just concentrate on putting your leg over the fence," Blaze said gently, to help calm her down. She tried to pull her right leg over, but her shorts got caught. Suddenly, she felt a sharp sting in her inner thigh. Her body started to shake, enough to rattle the gate.

"Okay, okay, just calm down, you got it. Now, turnaround and climb down," Blaze said. Seanette got herself together, pulled her right leg safely over the gate and made her way down. She continued to follow Blaze as they ran across the school. There was another locked gate at the front of the school, which thankfully was just loosely padlocked. As she and Blaze easily slipped through, she was reminded about her childhood playtime with her friend Stacy back in Leimert Park, how they'd slip through the apartment gates during their made-up adventures.

Her thoughts were quickly interrupted by Blaze tugging at her arm. "Get down!" he warned, breathing hard from all the running as he pulled her behind some bushes for cover. "Lil' Insane just passed by in his car." Seanette peeked up over the bushes and saw Lil' Insane in his yellow Pinto wagon, blasting Too Short's "The Ghetto" as he drove recklessly down the street. "You got two more blocks, and you will be back home," Blaze whispered assuredly to her.

They hid in the bushes until he passed by, then they sprinted across the street. Blaze followed Seanette to make sure she made it safely as she ran the last two blocks to Debbie's porch. Immediately, the adrenaline left and the sharp sting returned aggressively to her right inner thigh. "You're bleeding!" Blaze exclaimed. She looked down at her thigh. Not only was she bleeding, but her shorts were torn all the way up to the inner seam line.

Debbie heard the commotion and came to the door. Blaze blurted out, "Aye, she' bleeding!" Debbie looked down at Seanette's leg, turned around, and went in the house to get some ointment. By the time she came back, Wana had made it home and was on the porch laughing about what happened. "That was crazy, huh? You alright?"

Seanette was upset. That was the last straw. She was ready to go home. She was over the 'hood. Period. "You better not tell your momma," Debbie said as she returned with the ointment and applied it to Seanette's thigh. "She'll never let you come back." "That's a given," Seanette thought to herself. After everything, she had no intentions of returning. Besides, Dom still hadn't come yet, and there was no sign of him ever showing up. She was just glad the break was over.

The one thing that puzzled her, though, was why Lil' Insane assaulted her. She wasn't his girlfriend, and they never even talked let alone dated. She didn't even like him. Later, she learned from Blaze that Lil' Insane was high on PCP that night.

Transparent

Under the ocean
Beneath the sea
Inevitably is where you will find me
Floating through all space and time
My emotions and pain trail me close behind
Under the ocean
Beneath the sea
Where the worries of this world have engulfed me

CHAPTER 27

In the Jaws of Death

While everyone seemed so enthusiastic about all the twelfth-grade festivities, Seanette was dreading the fact that second semester had started and she still had not passed the math portion of the HSCE test. On top of that, she was uninterested in senior pictures, prom and graduation, especially since she had not seen or talked to Dom in almost a year-and-a-half.

Seanette simply stopped caring about everything as a result of her deepening depression. She arrived at school in her pajamas and house shoes, and her hair was unkempt. She didn't care that the once "cool crowd" she hung out with clowned her. She wanted to die. She still wrote her "Dear Father God" letters, but they all said the same things: "I hate life. I want to die."

On top of that, her mother and Charles were deeper in their addiction, and they were still fighting and arguing all the time. Plus, food began to be scarcer in the house, but Seanette stopped calling Diane. In fact, she just stopped eating. She had no appetite. She was actually surprised that her once dear companion that had previously given her instant gratification, enjoyment and comfort suddenly became an arch-enemy that left her constantly agitated. That's how much her depression consumed her every fiber.

Seanette did her best to prepare herself mentally to take the HSCE test again. She got the results back pretty quickly from her counselor, and her heart sank when she learned she did not pass yet again. After this, she only had one last chance to pass and receive her high school diploma. She felt completely helpless. Needless to say, she didn't have the courage to tell her mother, so she was determined to keep it a secret for as long as she could. Pam was the last thing she wanted to deal with.

Leaving her counselor's office, as Seanette shuffled down the hallway, she saw a crowd gathered by the lockers. She spotted an acquaintance, who had allowed her to store her books, talking loudly and pointing in her direction. When Seanette approached, the girl said, "I'm so glad you showed up. When are you going to get your stuff out of my locker? This is not a storage." Her attitude stunned Seanette. She then threw all of Seanette's books on the floor.

Seanette watched emotionless, and she didn't say a word. She just picked up her books and walked away. "That was messed up," she heard someone say to the girl. "Hmph, I don't care," the girl retorted. Seanette walked out of the building and onto the courtyard. From that day forward, she sat by herself. During lunch and in between periods, a few people spoke to her as they walked by, and she soon found good friends in Wayne, Mia and Emma.

Wayne and Seanette's common bond was music. He was a black kid in a tagging crew. Mia and Emma were sisters and were Armenian. Both girls were beautiful inside and out. Mia treated Seanette like a sister from day one and they formed an instant bond. She didn't care about the way Seanette dressed, her hair or her weight. She loved her for her. She was such a good soul and very selfless. She was so giving, caring, kind, loving and genuine. And her sister Emma was so animated with her stories and so exuberant. She was the life of the party and made Seanette laugh. The three of them rapped and sang together, laughed and cried together. They completed each other's sentences. They were like the Three Musketeers and hung out together every day.

The last HSCE test date approached and Seanette felt defeated before she even took it. Her mother found out about her failing the last go-round and pretty much gave her a death threat! No surprise there. Seanette was over it. Although she was very nervous, she had gotten to the point of just going through the motions.

As she entered the cafeteria, her eyes scanned the room. It was full, with very few empty chairs. This elevated her anxiety. She grabbed an answer sheet, two #2 pencils and a testing booklet from the counselors' table. Then she found a seat and tried to calm her mind and fears.

One of the counselors stood up, laid down the ground rules and started the timer. Seanette opened the booklet and let out a heavy sigh. Her spirit sank as she glanced at the questions. Profuse sweat began to form on her brows and forehead and she started to quietly cry. Discreetly wiping the tears away with her shirt, she randomly filled in option "C" along the answer sheet for the first question. Really, she didn't read any of the questions because she didn't understand them, let alone know how to solve the problems.

When she was done, Seanette laid her hand on her answer sheet and whispered a quick prayer, "God, if you are real, please help me pass this test." She turned in her materials to the counselor and walked out of the cafeteria.

A few days later, Seanette found out she passed!

With some hope in life restored, so was Seanette's interest in going to the prom. Since Dom apparently wasn't available, she decided to ask her new friend Wayne to go. He was cool with her, and she felt safe with him. Mia was excited about the prom, too, and took Seanette to get her nails and hair done. Even her mother and Diane got involved, chipping in to pay for the prom tickets, Seanette's dress and shoes, a limousine and a rental car. (They also paid for her senior portraits and class ring.) And Wayne got her a corsage. Seanette had a genuinely good time at the prom, as she and Wayne danced and clowned around with Mia.

After the prom, Seanette drove the rental car with Wayne to pick up a couple of burgers and chill, and then she dropped him off at his mother's house. It was quaint and simple. She felt no pressure. Wayne was a gentleman and her friend and she savored the experience as she drove off.

Otis died that year. His funeral was oddly quiet, and Diane didn't even cry during the services. The entire situation was really pretty morbid. As usual, no one talked about his passing, and beyond the funeral, everyone just kept going on with life like nothing happened.

Graduation day finally came and Seanette's mother, Diane, Aunt Regina, and cousins Desi and Angel were all at the ceremony. Just as soon as the day came, it left, along with the rest of the year. Seanette didn't have a concrete plan as to what to do with her life after high school. With no goals or any ambition for the future, she just sort of drifted and got lost in the shuffle. Frankly, she couldn't see further than her current circumstance, so she did what she knew best—she worked. Since the age of fourteen, she got jobs through the summer youth program that helped at-risk youth of lower socio-economic status. Both she and Wayne got many job assignments through the program, which gave her enough experience to compile a decent resume and secure gainful employment at the local movie theater, a retail store and a bakery in the mall.

Seanette also started taking some classes at a community college. But the truth was, she really wasn't ready for school again. Besides, there was another problem brewing. Seanette started smoking marijuana again, and this time with her mother and Charles. Every day. Her friends, sisters Mia and Emma, were also there every day, smoking with them. Pam didn't care if they smoked weed, as long as they shared it with her.

Pam and Charles still had a love-hate relationship, partly because his behavior was so unpredictable. He was so hard to read, and his emotions could flip on and off like a light switch.

One of the worst instances was the day he decided to take Pam, Seanette and his grandchildren to the zoo. It was the first and last outing they had as a family. The whole day had gone perfectly. Everyone got along and had a great time. Charles even purchased a disposable camera for them to take pictures.

When they were all ready to go home, Charles rounded up everyone to the car and drove his grandchildren to their parents first. Then they stopped at the liquor store for him to buy a half pint of liquor, which he drank while driving back to the Valley. All of a sudden, he started driving erratically and cursing out Pam. He then pulled over to the shoulder of the freeway and yelled at Pam and Seanette to get out of the car. Pam told Seanette to go ahead and get out and when they did, Charles threw the disposable camera out the window and sped off.

Pam started throwing accusations at Seanette, blaming her for Charles' behavior. "You better find us a ride home. This is all your fault. Hurry up and walk faster." The cold of the night and the wind from the cars zooming by sent chills up Seanette's back as they walked down the off-ramp. Mia was the only person she knew to call. After consoling Seanette, who was crying as she told Mia what happened, Mia consoled her without any judgment and immediately picked them up. Pam did not utter a word all the way home.

When they got there, Charles was sitting on the couch with all the lights off. He forgot his key and had broken the window to get in. He got up to confront Pam, but Seanette couldn't believe he had the audacity to be there after kicking them of out the car on the freeway. Pam told her to go to her room, but Seanette stood her ground. Not just to him but to her mother, as well. "No, I'm not going anywhere. You're not going to make him leave? He needs to leave now."

"Shut up and mind your business!" Charles responded. "Momma, look at what he did to our window!" Seanette yelled as her mother just stood there silent and motionless. "So what? I'll tear up everything in here," Charles threatened. "You don't believe me? Huh? Watch me!" He marched into the kitchen and rummaged around until he found a glass. He filled the glass with water, came back into the living room, went over to the VCR that sat on top of the television, and poured the water into it. That VCR was the last tangible, physical representation of Christopher, who bought it about six months before his death.

This set Seanette off. Enraged, she went into the kitchen, opened the dishwasher and picked up the biggest knife she could see, then returned to the living room waving the knife at Charles. "I said get out! Now!" Pam suddenly snapped out of her trance. She opened the door and picked up the steel baseball bat they kept on the front porch. Charles fled the scene, temporarily. He went on one of his "vacations" but, as usual, sooner or later came back. And, as usual, he was welcomed back in despite no apology, and the dynamics of the house went back to "normal."

It was at this time that Seanette decided to go live with her father Sean for a while. She had been in telephone contact with him and he told her he was approved for subsidized housing at a senior citizens apartment building on Los Angeles' westside. She asked if she could come live with him and he was elated, telling her she could stay as long as she wanted. Seanette was excited, too. Finally, she was going to live with her father. She didn't have suitcases, so she packed her clothes in grocery bags. She didn't care. She just wanted to get out of her mother's house.

Seanette took the bus to get to her father's house. At the end of her ride, she spotted him standing at the bus stop. They hugged each other, then laughed and talked while they walked to his apartment. Seanette didn't know what to expect with his place. He warned her that his apartment was small but said he was in the process of getting approved for a bigger one. Seanette didn't care. She just longed to be with him. He could have told her he lived in a trash can and she would've copped a squat right next to him anyway.

Sean's building looked worn. The paint was a weathered, dull orange color. A small crowd of people hanging around outside greeted Sean as he and Seanette walked up. He proudly introduced his daughter the same way he used to do when she was little. She smiled big and proud, gloating in the moment. They entered the glass double doors, and he led the way to the elevator. The building smelled of stale cigarettes and medicated cream. It was definitely old, Seanette thought to herself. Sean pressed the button for the second floor and there were rickety noises coming from the elevator shaft. They got out of the elevator and Sean stopped at the third apartment on the right. The door barely opened and Seanette realized it was because there was a twin bed right behind it.

Seanette quickly scanned her father studio apartment. Sean had piles of clothes in a corner, a thirteen-inch TV on a TV stand, a small dinette table, a small kitchen area and a small bathroom all in his five hundred square foot home. He was clearly embarrassed, constantly saying he was moving soon. Again, Seanette didn't care. She was just glad to finally have one of her parents to herself.

Initially, Sean cooked everyday for Seanette. He soon noticed she wasn't eating very much and asked her about it, commenting on how much weight she had lost. Seanette shrugged it off and always changed the subject every time he brought it up.

Their daily itinerary was always the same: get up, smoke a cigarette, walk to the weed spot, smoke out on the way back, play cards and dominoes for the rest of the day, and cook. Sean taught Seanette how to make smothered steak, greens and hot water cornbread. He would serenade his daughter with singing and rapping as he cooked. She listened and smiled as he sang along in perfect pitch to Tony Toni Tone's "Anniversary" or Xscape's "Just Kickin' It," or stumbled through the lyrics as he rapped to "U Don't Hear Me Tho'" by Rodney-O and Joe Cooley. Seanette was in charge of rolling the marijuana. She really liked the high of smoking weed. It took her mind away from everything and it relaxed her, and it suppressed her appetite.

Soon, though, as much as she enjoyed getting high with her father, this lifestyle grew old to Seanette. She wanted to go places and do things with him, which he always promised to do but never followed through. Instead, he began leaving her in the apartment alone. It started off with him telling her he was "going to the store" and would be right back. Seanette knew exactly what that meant.

She started searching for clues and ransacked the bathroom drawers when he was gone. Sure enough, she found a homemade glass crack pipe and a broken-off piece of a wire hanger, which she knew was used as a pusher. She was devastated.

Her father's behavior soon became erratic. He was always paranoid and questioning her about her mother. Pam had started to call more frequently and, at first, Seanette was annoyed and thought she was being a helicopter mom. But then she realized her mother had legitimate concerns about Sean's power of influence over her. It wasn't long before Seanette left her father's house after a falling out when he was high. She didn't even say goodbye. She just took all of her belongings and caught the bus home. Pam never asked what happened, and Seanette was glad.

Seanette's marijuana use increased dramatically when she returned from living with her father. She continued to lose more weight and was in a constant state of despair. She continued to cry out to God for help in her "Dear Father God" letters, but He didn't seem to respond. In fact, things seemed to be getting worse between her, Pam and Charles.

Then it looked as if things were starting to turn around. Aunt Regina and Desi came over for a barbecue one day. Desi kept watching Seanette the entire time, but she didn't say a word. Two days later, Diane called and invited Seanette to a church picnic that coming Saturday, so Seanette spent the weekend over Diane's house. At the picnic, she helped Diane and the other mothers of the church set up and also laughed and talked with the teenagers there. She actually felt normal and was able to talk to the kids with ease, which really surprised her about herself. After services on Sunday, during church dinner in the fellowship hall, Seanette again interacted well with the kids. She felt so comfortable, as if she had been there in that setting before.

After the church dinner, when Diane dropped her off back at Pam's, before Seanette got out of the car, Diane asked her, "'Nette, what are you going to do with your life?" Seanette was surprised. She didn't know what to say. She replied as honestly as she could, "I don't know." "Would you come stay with me if I offered?" Seanette immediately answered, "Yes."

The next few days brought dramatic changes for Seanette. For one, she decided to stop smoking marijuana and promised herself to never smoke it again. She also decided one day to start reading the Bible, but she didn't know how to read it or where to start, and she didn't understand the translation she had at all. The next day, a neighbor invited her to a church revival and Seanette accepted. She was desperate and she needed answers. She wanted to hear from God because, from her perspective, He had been silent for so long. She was not going to miss this opportunity to hear Him speak directly to her about her life.

When Seanette got to the church, she purposely sat by an older lady who appeared to be a mother of the church. This brought her comfort and made her think of her Aunt Joy. She instantly felt peace when she sat next to the lady, who looked at her and smiled. As the service went on, this sweet woman slipped Seanette a piece of paper with the scripture Isaiah 40:31 written on it, which says, "But those who hope in the Lord will renew their strength. They will soar on wings like eagles; they will run and not grow weary, they will walk and not be faint."

(New International Version) Seanette tucked the paper in her back pocket and quietly cried.

When the pastor called an altar call, Seanette went up for prayer and said she wanted to rededicate her life to the Lord. The pastor anointed her head with oil and prayed. She said the Lord had a high calling for Seanette's life, which was to work with the youth. He would use her to touch many lives, and He had heard her cry. Seanette became so overtaken with emotion, she couldn't contain herself. She wailed and cried loudly, and then she prayed to the Lord and promised to submit to His will.

Once she got home from church, Seanette immediately called Diane and asked if her offer was still open. Immediately, Diane came to pick Seanette up. Seanette and her mother did not exchange goodbyes. Pam just closed the door behind her.

New Beginnings

On a journey to a place
So grateful for mercy and grace
On the trail, search to see
If I can find all of what's
Truly inside me
On a mission to heal my soul
I'm tired of reaching for things and people
To make me feel whole
On a quest
Learning how to love myself
Instead of putting my dreams
And goals on a shelf
Leaving behind the hurts of my past
All the meaningless things I knew
In my heart would not last
Reminding myself to take one day at a time
Besides
It's the real me
I'm searching to find

CHAPTER 28

Blessed Assurance

L iving with Diane was a breath of fresh air for Seanette. One of the first things Diane did was take her shopping for new clothes, since she had lost so much weight. Diane spent at least three thousand dollars on both church and everyday wear for Seanette, along with undergarments, pajamas, shoes, purses, jewelry and accessories. In and out of malls across the San Fernando Valley they went. Seanette was very grateful.

She had gone from a size 14/16 to a size 6/8. This was the smallest she had ever been in her life, so it was drastic for her. She couldn't believe it. She tried to embrace her new body, but her low self-esteem impeded her and she still saw herself as overweight when she looked in the mirror. She just couldn't get past the negative thoughts that played like a tape recorder in her head.

Seanette knew Diane would require her to go to church every week and get involved. Diane retired when Otis died the previous year, and now she was dedicating most of her time to her church. She held several positions in the office auxiliaries, including membership on the Mother, Deaconess, Missionary, Pastor, Lay and Stewardess Board, and the Prayer and Bible Band. And she helped prepare, cook and serve the church dinners in the fellowship hall every Sunday. Seanette admired her dedication to serving the Lord. The only other person she knew who was as dedicated to God was Aunt Joy. Now, she was eager to get involved herself. Besides becoming a junior missionary, she joined the choir right away because it was something she had always enjoyed. She was in the youth choir at Aunt Joy's church and took a choir class at North Point School. Besides that, at Diane's church she was able to form real friendships with the other choir members.

Also, the pastor encouraged Seanette to work in the Youth People's Department. She worked alongside Theo, a college student who was committed to working with the youth on breaks from school up north. Theo and his fiancé Tammy attended the same college, and both were fully on fire for God. Seanette admired their passion. Theo was very transparent about his experiences, struggles, challenges and triumphs as a young man who truly loved the Lord.

Seanette got along well with the kids at church. She took pride in learning about the Bible and creating fun and engaging lesson plans for the youth. To help them learn the books of the Bible, she created a rap song that was easy to remember and recite. She even collaborated with another choir member to put on a play with the youth at the local community center. She wrote the entire script. The youth and other adults pulled together and helped with the sets and the designs. It was a huge success! Seanette thrived off of being a part of something bigger than her. It gave her hope and encouragement. She was starting to believe her best days were yet to come.

Diane told Seanette to focus primarily on school and church and not to worry about getting a job. This surprised Seanette and she didn't want Diane to think she was taking advantage of her while she was still trying to figure out what to do with her life. She wanted to help out and do her part. So, she did what she knew best, which was complying with whatever Diane said or asked for, whenever she said it or asked for it.

She also listened to Diane's wisdom about life and the lessons she learned. For instance, Diane gave her pocket money every month from her recycled cans and showed her how to budget her money. She even gave her Otis's old car. And when Diane noticed that she wasn't really eating—Seanette had developed a fear of food and was scared to eat—she began educating her on how to eat healthy foods. In return,

Seanette showed gratitude by cleaning up after herself and around the house.

Plus, she spent time with Diane. They prayed together. They laughed together. They watched the news and movies together. They drank coffee and talked through the night together. They exercised together. They took long walks through the neighborhood together. Seanette enjoyed spending time with Diane and appreciated everything Diane did for her.

Diane suggested Seanette enroll in the local adult school and take courses related to the medical field, such as medical terminology, billing, employment preparation and training. Although Seanette didn't really have an interest in the medical field, she took the classes anyway. In the meantime, she had a growing interest in working with children. She just didn't know what classes to take or where to go. When she expressed this interest to Diane, Diane just scoffed. "You will never make any money being a social worker."

"It's not about the money," Seanette thought to herself. She just wanted to help kids. She felt she could relate to them and wanted to share her story and her experiences. Money? She would have done it for free! Sure, Diane meant well, but Seanette wanted to pursue a career that she loved. Maybe she didn't know much, but she knew she had a passion for the youth.

Seanette made the decision that, after completing all the medical field courses at the adult school, she would get information as to what classes would qualify her to work with youth. She didn't know in what capacity, but it felt right to her soul to talk to kids and listen to them. Upon completion of her course work, Seanette was placed in a temporary position in the medical records department at the local county hospital through an employment agency. Diane tried to persuade her to seek permanent employment there, but while Seanette was grateful for the job, in her soul she felt out of place and was just going through the motions.

Through casual conversation with someone at church, Seanette learned she could meet with a counselor at the local community college to find out all of the required courses she needed to pursue her desired career. Seanette made plans to meet with the counselor and enroll in classes the upcoming semester.

Then, in a twist of fate, when her assignment through the employment agency was finished, the county decided not to renew her contract. She was partially relieved but also overwhelmed. "Now what?"

Yes, Seanette wanted to go to college. But her heart sank as soon as the counselor told her she would be required to pass math. That familiar fear and defeat creep back into her heart. She just thanked the counselor and left. Back at Diane's house, she grabbed the classified section of the newspaper and looked for a job. She did this relentlessly every day. Still, it didn't take long for her to start feeling like a failure. Even with her diligent job search, she had too much downtime and needed to find something to do.

Diane suggested Seanette volunteer at the local senior center while she looked for a job. One of the mothers of the church, Mrs. Nelson, was the head volunteer there, and Seanette formed an instant bond with her. Ms. Nelson was a very active volunteer for someone who was eighty-six years old. She was always busy and helping others. She ran circles around the director, assistor director, the other volunteers, even Seanette. She did so many different things for the center but never sought recognition.

She was also witty and made Seanette laugh. Ms. Nelson was a ray of sunshine to everyone who came into contact with her. Seanette in particular found her easy to talk to because she listened and was supportive. Her advice was always sound while also urging Seanette to make up her own mind. Seanette was glad to volunteer.

Seanette shared with Ms. Nelson that she wanted to work with children. Ms. Nelson wasn't surprised. "Well, baby, if that's what you want, then go on ahead and do it," she encouraged her. "You are smart as a whip! You can do it. You can do anything you put your mind to. You're going to be great. I just know it. I can feel it. Keep God first, and you will make it all the way to the top." Seanette never had anyone say those words to her. Tears welled up in her eyes. She was overwhelmed with love. That day, she decided to focus on a job working with youth.

This plan did not go over well with Diane. She told Seanette she was wasting her time. When Seanette stood her ground, Diane told her to leave her home. So, with nowhere else to go, after a year of living with Diane, Seanette went back to her mother's house. She was twenty years old.

Misunderstood

Oh, Lord . . .
I thought I heard
You call me by name
In my darkest hour
I felt you nudge my hand
"Go forth," YOU SAID
I am confused
I feel lost
I feel alone
Familiar spirits dance around me
They mock me
They laugh at me
They ridicule me
They blame me
They taunt me
Constantly
I just want a love to call my own
I just want my own family
I yell from my core
I will make the rules
I will do it my way
This time
On my own

CHAPTER 29
Ground Zero

Seanette was not particularly happy about returning to her mother's house. Pam immediately started asking for money. Seanette was constantly going to the ATM.

Seanette was so frustrated. The life she experienced with Diane was a dream compared to this. Her anger started rising to the surface again, including with God. She felt it must be her destiny for the odds to be stacked up against her. She could not wrap her head around how she ended up back where she began.

"Okay, well, forget it," she resigned in her mind. "I'll just get high." When she told her mother to call the weed man, Pam was mildly reluctant but eventually called him. Seanette remembered her promise to herself to never smoke marijuana again. But that was short-lived. She wanted a release. She felt trapped, like there was no other way out. This was her future and she accepted it. She could feel herself growing numb.

The weed man came and left. Pam cleaned the marijuana (separated the seeds from the buds) and rolled a joint. She took a long toke and passed it to Seanette. Seanette grabbed it and slowly inhaled long and slow. As soon as she did, she couldn't shake the feeling of knowing this was wrong for her. Not to mention the fact that the weed wasn't having the desired effect. She wasn't getting high! The only thing that happened was all of the hurt, pain, anger, confusion, and loneliness were intensified. Puzzled by this, she gave the joint back to her mother and went upstairs to use the phone.

She called her friend Theo from the youth ministry. In spite of her anger towards God about having to be back with her mother and that environment, she was still pouring her heart into the church and those children. She told Theo exactly what happened. He listened, offered her place to stay, and she was in his and Tammy's house that same day. Theo and Tammy had gotten married, and they were expecting their first child. Seanette was so appreciative of them both.

They said Seanette could stay as long as she wanted to, and she was grateful, but she felt out of place in their home. She still struggled severely with her self-esteem and couldn't believe they were willing to help her. She had a hard time accepting love. So, after two days, she wrote a nice thank you note and left. After that, she sometimes stayed with her mother but also couch surfed at friends' houses while she continued to look for a job.

The house she stayed at the most was Wayne's. Since his mother and Pam got high together, Seanette felt it would be better to be around someone who could relate to her issues at home. She felt safe with him. Wayne didn't smoke or drink, and he was a positive influence on her. She soon started working as a child care worker at a group home, a job she loved because she was back working with children. She was twenty-one years old.

Wayne's mother didn't seem bothered that Seanette spent the night. At first, their relationship was platonic. They went to the movies together and listened to music in his room like when they were in high school. After a while, though, they began dating and having sex. Seanette didn't feel comfortable having sex in Wayne's mother's house, so she found an apartment. She told Wayne he was free to stay with his mother's, but he insisted they were going to be together and live as a couple.

Seanette was over the moon! She finally had her own place and her own family, and her own rules. No one could tell her what to do. Not even God. And she didn't have to ask permission about anything. She could dance to the beat of her own drum. She worked overtime to earn enough money to decorate the apartment and to replenish her bank account, which had dwindled when she lived with Pam.

Seanette decided to head back to school after the new year. But until then, it was still just the beginning of summer and she wanted to have some fun before hitting the books. Wayne got a job at a grocery store, and things couldn't be better. Seanette and Wayne barely saw one another, though. She worked double shifts, and he worked swing. If they did see each other, it was brief, or they were in transition (to bed, showering, or eating).

Wayne had a secret he neglected to tell Seanette before he moved in. One day he casually mentioned that he had fathered a daughter a year before they got together. When she pressed him for information as to her whereabouts, he was very guarded. Seanette wanted to meet her. She felt if they were going to be together, she wanted to know and love his daughter, too. Wayne blamed his daughter's mother for the estranged relationship between him and his child. Since he seemed angry every time Seanette asked, she stopped bringing it up.

Summer came and went, and Seanette increased her hours at the group home. Unfortunately, the more she worked, the further she and Wayne drifted away from each other. There was a growing disconnect between them, and something was different that she couldn't quite put her finger on. But she shrugged it off, thinking she was just being paranoid. She was emotional by nature and figured her emotions were all over the place because she had no balance with all the hours she was working.

In fact, she was working so many hours that she didn't even notice she had missed her period. It usually came like clockwork the first week of every month, but this time it was almost the third week before she realized it hadn't come. The pregnancy stunned her. She and Wayne used condoms early on, and then they got lazy and comfortable with each other and just stopped. But still, it caught them both by surprise.

Seanette immediately called her mother and Diane to tell them. Well, Pam was very upset and hung up on her. Diane told her she needed to get married as soon as possible and then hung up. Seanette told Wayne how they reacted to the news and what Diane said about getting married. He was really indifferent about it.

Wishing for the best, Seanette went ahead and purchased a gold band for Wayne at the local pawn shop and proposed to him the following week. He agreed, and Diane offered to buy her wedding dress. A few days after Christmas, they were married by the pastor who baptized Seanette when she was a child. The only other people there were two friends from high school, who served as the witnesses. That was it. There was no party, no celebration. The marriage was just a formality.

Eight days later, Wayne said, pretty matter of factly, that he wanted a divorce. The only explanation he offered was that things were not the same since they got married. Seanette was devastated. She had trusted Wayne, she felt safe with him. He was the last person she thought would abandon her.

Wayne immediately moved back in with his mother. Seanette later found out through his cousin that Wayne was using her car to go to his daughter's mother's house. He denied it when Seanette confronted him about this, but then soon thereafter, he moved in with the mother. Seanette didn't see him or hear from him until the divorce proceedings. Diane paid for a fancy-pants divorce attorney on Ventura Blvd., but they couldn't get an annulment because the marriage was consummated. Seanette was shattered.

But that didn't stop her from focusing on her child. She worked even more assertively as she prepared for the baby's arrival. Also, as a result of her and Diane talking more frequently, Diane went with her to every doctor's appointment. Her mother, on the other hand, was nowhere to be found. In fact, Seanette did not see her until the baby shower, which Diane hosted at her house. Pam took the opportunity to brag to everyone there that she had purchased the baby's crib, walker and dresser. Not that Seanette wasn't grateful. She just wanted to have her mother be a more active part of this whole experience.

Seanette was so lonely and depressed in her apartment by herself. Even though she was working so much and was hardly home, it was a constant reminder of Wayne abandoning her, especially when she was pregnant with his child. So, Diane proposed that she move back in with her. Diane would help with babysitting, and besides, it didn't make sense for her to work so hard to pay for an apartment she was hardly in. After the way things turned out the last time, though, Seanette was very apprehensive about it. But Diane had a point. Seanette could save some money and make a more thorough plan for her and her baby. So, she moved back in with her.

Noah arrived in the heat of August. He was perfect. Diane and Pam were both there at the delivery, but Wayne did not show up until two days later. He hadn't shown any interest in his child or help pay for anything in preparation for the baby's arrival, which deeply vexed Seanette. She had to call his mother to let her know his baby was born. The conversation between Wayne and Seanette was awkward and brief, and he didn't stay long. While he met his son, Seanette just stared off as she tried to grasp that she was a mother, that at twenty-two years old she was now responsible for a life, for life.

Young and Reckless

I close my eyes
Breathe deep within
Throwing caution
To the wind
With an open heart
I jump right in
Drawn to the fire
In your eyes
I am mesmerized
Like a magnet
Your energy draws me near
I am hypnotized
By all the hidden mysteries
Your tattooed body reveals
I am intrigued
Compelled to solve and heal
Avoiding the road signs
Which point to danger unforeseen
My own insecurities
Erode my low self-esteem
This chance
I am willing to take
Therefore I do not hesitate
Falling in love
With you

CHAPTER 30
Auto Pilot

L iving back at Diane's house presented more issues than Seanette had bargained for. In fact, she knew it was a mistake the moment she moved in. She knew Diane meant well, but Diane was very controlling, especially when it came to Noah. Whether it was diapers, wipes, clothes, food, toys or the latest gadgets, Diane purchased it first, before Seanette had an opportunity to provide for her own son. On top of that, she criticized everything Seanette did with him. Seanette couldn't do anything right.

She tried to seek refuge and solace at church, but Diane had told everyone that she had mental health issues. She continued to attend but felt judged, and she struggled with understanding God's love because her life seemed to be in shambles. To make matters worse, Wayne was not adhering to the court orders on child support and visitation. He didn't pay, and he rarely came to see his son.

Motherhood was something Seanette was not prepared for. As an only child, she had no experience with babies and so didn't understand them or their constant needs. Sure, she had been around her younger cousin Tiffany (Bruce's daughter) as a baby, but that was primarily on the weekends, and she didn't provide constant care for her. She really didn't have much experience with Tiffany until Tiffany was about three years old and already pretty self-sufficient. By then, she could talk, walk, feed herself and use the toilet by herself, and was always fun to be around.

Seanette soon realized she had no patience with Noah. She was so exhausted all the time and easily frustrated.

But compounding the angst of new motherhood was the fact that Seanette was very angry. She was angry with herself for having a baby without being prepared, for not finishing college, and for having just a job and not a career. And she was angry because she hated feeling like she was a bad mother.

Seanette also hated Wayne. She felt betrayed. She felt he left her holding the bag. She felt like he got away and went on with his life. Whenever she did speak with him (usually via telephone), they always had some big blowup and one of them usually ended up hanging up on the other. She was always overwhelmed, constantly cried about her situation, and every day she prayed for strength and wisdom.

Fortunately, these feelings did not immobilize her. She continued to work overtime, getting to the point where she basically lived temporarily at the group home while Diane watched Noah. Seanette greeted the children at the start of her morning shift, then worked through a second shift until it was time to bid them good night. Then, she slept in the therapist's office and, when she woke up, she showered before her next morning shift and started all over again.

This work schedule meant that Diane practically raised Noah for the first year-and-a-half of his life. Seanette had mixed feelings about this. On the one hand, she had peace of mind that he was safe and well taken care of, and she really appreciated not having to worry about childcare or him leaving his home environment. On the other hand, she wanted to experience all of Noah's milestones by herself, without the constant commentary from Diane. She also wanted him to have a good transition into a preschool where he could learn and grow and gain invaluable social skills. The only way she saw that happening was to work towards a plan to move out of Diane's house. And this time, for good.

To some degree, though, Seanette's feelings at this point were conflicted. Motherhood had taken a serious toll on her as a person and she wanted a break. A break from life, from Noah, from work, from everything. She just wanted to be young and free. After all, she was only twenty-two years old. She wanted to explore and embrace life. She didn't want to be identified as someone's mother, daughter, employee or even friend. She wanted to feel desirable and attractive.

She wanted to be a woman, to be catered to and looked after. She wanted to be loved. All in all, she just wanted to be a regular person. She was tired of being bogged down with this never-ending stream of stresses in her life, feeling like for every two steps forward, she always had to make up those two steps plus add on five more.

Around this time, Diane's brother got deathly ill, so she volunteered to take Noah with her up north while she helped his wife. Seanette felt like she had gotten her freedom papers. As soon as Diane and her son headed north, Seanette hit the freeway heading south, straight to Los Angeles.

Her first stop was Joy's house. She really missed her. It was so good to see her. Of course, it bothered Seanette that everyone asked about Noah when she was trying to enjoy her freedom. But she pushed her feelings to the side and proudly showed off her latest photos of him in her wallet and bragged about his "monumental" milestones.

Some of Joy's nieces were going to visit her younger sister Janet and Janet's longtime boyfriend James. Seanette was excited to see them. They were the fun, popular, young couple that Seanette and all the kids always wanted to be around she was younger. She couldn't remember the last time she had seen them, guessing it must have been when she was about fifteen years old. She reflected on how so much had changed so quickly for her since then. She got in her car and headed over.

When she got to Janet's house, parked and jumped out of the car, she noticed him quietly sitting on a bike in the courtyard of their apartment complex. He was dressed in all black—black hoodie, black pants and black tennis shoes. Seanette felt a breeze blow her freshly flat-ironed, long, black hair across her cheek. Her hair grew like weeds down to the middle of her back when she was pregnant with Noah. She had on a cream-colored pullover sweater, fitted ripped jeans and boots. He quickly caught her attention as he studied her. She studied him, too. "This is a different approach to courtship," she mused. She was immediately captivated by him even though she didn't even know his name or who he was. Soon enough, she found out he was James's nephew Jayden, or "JJ."

JJ was a notorious active gang member. He had been in and out of juvenile hall, the California Youth Authority and had just completed a two-and-a-half-year prison term for bank robbery. His body was covered everywhere with tattoos—people often joked that he looked like a walking newspaper. He was the total polar opposite of Wayne, Dom and Pretty Boy. Sure, two out of those three had been involved in gangs and drugs and served some jail time. But JJ was in a class of his own, and she wanted to try something new.

Frankly, it didn't take long for Seanette to think that maybe JJ was her soulmate. Besides being very charismatic, he was quite attentive and always wanted to be around her and take care of her. He always had money and didn't mind spending it on her or giving her some.

Determined to make this relationship work, Seanette put all her effort into JJ. She stopped working overtime, and on her days off, she was in Los Angeles at Aunt Janet's house.

JJ had a plan. He told her he wanted to marry her and have more babies. First, he wanted to meet Noah and insisted she drive up north to get him from Diane. He promised to help her with him and kept his promise by buying him some of the things he needed and helping with childcare expenses. Moreover, they spent time together and went places together like the park and the beach. This made Seanette feel special. They were a family.

At one point, Seanette moved out of Diane's house and moved in with Janet and James just so she could be closer to JJ. She wanted to be with him all the time. Other people teased her for being "so sprung on him." He would just laugh and wink at her. He knew he had her.

JJ was the first person she had sex with since being pregnant with Noah. He called her his queen the first time they had sex and told her he knew she was "the one." It really didn't bother her too much when she started to notice he was a bit controlling and wanted to know where she went and who she went with. She was flattered that he cared so much. No other guy paid that much attention to her. So she welcomed it with open arms.

Seanette and JJ dated through the summer. But then she broke up with him when she found out he was cheating on her. Shortly thereafter, JJ "hit a lick," meaning he robbed another bank, and was sentenced to four years in prison. Although she was saddened by this news—the last thing she wanted was for JJ to go to jail—she knew she needed to take this opportunity to get her life together. She was twenty-three years old and Noah was thirteen months.

Seanette found an apartment in Van Nuys, but it wouldn't be ready to rent for at least a month. So, she stayed at Diane's house in the meantime. She enrolled in the local community college and put Noah in daycare, the cost of which the college subsidized as long as she took classes and passed. The daycare was a Godsend because it was open twenty-four hours, which accommodated her crazy work schedule and still allowed her to complete eighteen units of classes each semester. She worked forty hours in three days and went to school the other days. She remained on the Dean's Honor Roll for three consecutive semesters and was even approached by a counselor to apply for a scholarship. Needless to say, she successfully completed all general education requirements—except math and science. She wouldn't even look at those classes in the course catalog each semester, deciding to leave them to the end.

Seanette and Noah lived a pretty low-key, almost reclusive existence, as her life revolved around taking care of him, working and going to school. She was still on the outs with her mother, who was still with Charles and in her addiction; and she would soon be on the outs with Diane.

About one week before Seanette's apartment was ready, Diane returned from up north. Seanette announced with excitement that she found her own place and was moving out. To her total, unpleasant surprise, Diane got very upset about it, seeming to take it personally.

In fact, Diane's reaction escalated quickly into physical violence, enough for neighbors to call the police. First, Diane and Seanette argued about her and Noah moving out. But when Seanette tried to leave, Diane suddenly took Noah out of her arms and refused to give him back. Seanette repeatedly told her to give him back, but Diane refused, so Seanette snatched him out of Diane's arms. Diane just kept warning her, "I'll take him from you! I'll take him from you!"

With Noah now in her arms, Seanette ran down the hall to the front door. But before she could get out, Diane pushed her into the front door and grabbed her by the throat, almost choking her. Seanette started sobbing as Noah wailed in her arms. With her hand still around Seanette's neck, Diane threatened her, "I will kill you and take this baby." At that, Seanette screamed at the top of her lungs and started reciting Psalm 23.

A neighbor approached their iron security door and asked if everything was alright. Diane quickly responded, "Yes, we are having a minor family dispute." But Seanette knew she had to seize the moment. So, she asked the neighbor not to leave. Diane squeezed her neck tighter and stomped on the top of her bare foot with her high heel, breaking the skin. The neighbor pleaded for Diane to open the door. She opened the door and let go of Seanette's neck, but then she grabbed her long ponytail and wrapped it around her hand to maintain a secure grip.

By now, Seanette had managed to get herself and Noah outside, with Diane still holding on to her hair. More neighbors were outside watching the unfolding scene. Seanette continued to make it down the walkway, to the driveway and toward the gate. All along, Diane held on to her hair. It was clear Diane was barely maintaining her cool. One of the oldest neighbors, Ms. Little, stood outside of the gate. "Diane, let the child go," she pleaded with a look of terror on her face. "She just wants to leave." "Fine, then leave," Diane said as she let go of Seanette's hair. But that wasn't enough. She told Seanette, "You ain't nothin' and you ain't never gonna amount to nothin'!"

Seanette was so confounded. As she stood on the curb, barefoot, with Noah on her hip, she rifled through her mind what to do. She felt so helpless. All of their belongings, clothes, shoes, diapers, food for Noah and their beds—everything they had was in Diane's house, including her purse. But Diane refused to let her take anything. Plus, Seanette didn't have anywhere to go. Her new apartment wouldn't be ready for at least another week. She and her baby were now homeless.

The next-door neighbors let Seanette use their phone. She called her mother at work and told her what happened. Pam seemed shocked and offered her home, but Seanette didn't want to return there. She then called Janet and James. They had moved from Los Angeles to the Valley, not too far away from Diane. Janet said she could stay with them until the new apartment was ready.

After making her calls, Seanette went back outside. Besides the street being filled with gawking neighbors, the police had arrived and were talking to the neighbor who had come to the door to help her. The neighbor pointed her out and an officer approached her.

The first question the officer asked was if she wanted to press charges against Diane. Seanette was offended. "No! Why would you ask me that?" He pointed out that her neck was bleeding from the deep scratches where Diane had choked her, and that the top of her foot had a gash that was bleeding and swollen where Diane had stomped on it. Seanette was too beside herself to notice until that moment.

Her attention was then drawn to the front of Diane's house where Diane was also being interviewed by a police officer. "Jail? What are you talking about?" Seanette heard her yell. "Look how big and fat she is and how small I am. You want to arrest me? You need to be arresting her!" The officer responded, "Ma'am, how did she get those scratches? Her shirt is torn, and her foot is bleeding. Did you assault her?" "Does it look like I assaulted her? This is my home. I am the victim here. She is crazy. Just look at her."

Seanette couldn't believe this was happening. She sobbed as she listened to Diane continue to tell her side of the story that blamed her for the entire thing. "Excuse me, Ma'am? Ma'am, do you want to press charges?" Seanette shifted her attention back to the officer who had interviewed her. "No, that's my granny. Of course not. I just want to get some of my things for me and my baby."

The police escorted Seanette back into Diane's house, and she quickly gathered her purse and as many personal items as she could. She had to leave behind her bed, Noah's car bed, the rest of their clothes, towels, shoes and mostly everything else. She loaded up her car and headed to Janet's and James' house. They welcomed her and Noah with open arms. They had a one-bedroom apartment and three kids, so Seanette had to make a pallet on the floor for herself and Noah. She didn't care. She just wanted to be safe.

The first thing Seanette did when she got to their house was take a shower. When she got out, she stared at herself in the mirror. As she took a good look at the bruises and cuts on her skin, she thought to herself, "I need a drastic change." She got dressed, grabbed a grocery bag and a pair of scissors from the kitchen and headed back to the bathroom. She parted her hair down the middle all the way to the back of her neck, grabbed one side at a time, and cut it. Just like that. Her long, beautiful, jet black hair that flowed to the middle of her back. She cut about nine inches off and was left with a short bob. Everyone in the house was shocked, but she didn't care. She had to do it. That hair was a curse, and she didn't want the bad vibes or the nightmares to haunt her ever again, especially after Diane had used it against her that day—literally.

One night during dinner, James casually brought up JJ. He said he was back in jail but would love to hear from Seanette. A year had gone by, and she wasn't mad at him anymore. The truth was, she missed him. She would daydream of him at school. She thought it couldn't hurt just to write him. She didn't respond when James mentioned JJ, but he did put him back on her mind. Two days later, she was asking for the address, and a day after that, she sent him a letter.

Seanette was so relieved when she got the call that her apartment was ready. There was just one problem. Diane was not very cooperative about allowing her to pick up her stuff. So, Seanette called one of the pastors of their church for help. Minister Washington was personable and everyone liked him, including Diane. He arranged to be present while Seanette got some more of her things, although she had to leave the beds and some other items behind. She and Noah slept on the floor of their new apartment, but thankfully, Janet gave her a care package filled with blankets, along with toiletries.

Seanette had to strategize how to get the rest of her and Noah's belongings. She tried to work it out with Diane through Minister Washington again, but he had to go out of town and was unavailable. Then one day, while she was visiting Janet, Janet's brother Jermaine and some of her nephews stopped by. They had heard what happened and offered to help. Jermaine was adamant about just going over to

Diane's house and getting the stuff out. Seanette didn't have her house key anymore, but Otis, Jr. was back at home from the mental hospital and Jermaine suggested, "It's a shot in the dark, but maybe he will help you out by opening the door?" Seanette knew the best time to go would be on Sunday when Diane would be in church until at least three o'clock. Janet offered to look after Noah while they helped Seanette move.

Sunday came and Seanette, Jermaine and all the nephews piled up in her car. She went to Otis' window and called his name. When he came to the front door, she asked if he would let her in so she could get the rest of her things. Otis looked her straight in the face and suddenly appeared coherent and alert. He was not in a trance or as heavily medicated as he usually was. "Yes, 'Nette, get all your stuff." They moved quickly as Jermaine told her to tie all her clothes and belongings in sheets. An onlooking neighbor saw her and asked if they could help, since they had a pickup truck. Seanette offered them twenty-five dollars to transport all her belongings to her new apartment. They agreed, and everyone continued to pile her belongings in her car and the truck.

Seanette was just loading up Noah's car bed when Diane pulled into the driveway. She immediately jumped out of her car. "Put everything back! You can't take nothing out of my house without my permission!" Seanette answered, "But it's all my stuff." "I don't care," Diane retorted. "Otis, why did you open the door? I told you not to open the door for anyone." Otis just stared blankly back at Diane. They continued loading the truck. "I don't want any trouble. I just want to get my stuff and leave!" Seanette cried. She got in her car, and the truck followed her to her new apartment.

That whole experience with Diane had a really negative impact on Seanette, especially regarding church. It would be several years before she would step back into one. She just stopped going and threw herself into school, work, Noah and JJ.

Unclaimed Baggage

*Forsaken
Shaking
Quivering
Spirit within
Contention
Petrified
Dreams blowing
In the wind
Facades and masquerades
Merry go round again*

CHAPTER 31
Playing with Fire

Seanette was so excited to move into her apartment. She swore she would never give up her independence to live with anyone ever again. She valued her freedom and wasn't going to live by anyone else's rules ever again. She still wasn't speaking to her mother or Diane, and that was just fine with her. She was determined to explore her freedom to the fullest without their influence or interference.

Seanette still attended college and worked at the group home, picking up a few hours of overtime here and there. It was a huge sacrifice for her to only work forty hours a week. At only $7.40 an hour, she constantly struggled with her finances. She couldn't even afford to pay her entire rent on time. Wayne was still nowhere to be found for child support. Thankfully, the manager allowed her to pay half the amount twice a month to coincide with her job's pay schedule.

Even though Seanette struggled to make ends meet, her main goal was to finish school. She had completed almost all her general education classes to transfer, but she still had to finish up her math, history and science requirements. She tried her best to take life in stride, considering that, for a twenty-four-year-old with a two-year-old, she was doing just fine.

JJ made a collect call to Seanette from jail every Saturday morning at ten o'clock without fail. She eagerly waited for his call before she did anything else. He was easy to talk to, and he kept her mind off the stress of everything in the "real world." Through the course of the year, in addition to the phone calls, they wrote each other three times a week.

Towards the end of 1998, JJ started asking Seanette to come see him. He was in prison up north, several hours away. Seanette agreed and asked Janet to keep Noah while she was gone. She had been approved for the visiting list for quite some time but didn't tell him because she planned to surprise him with a visit on his birthday. She dropped Noah off the night before and hit the road before the sun rose.

After clearing security, Seanette sat patiently in the visiting room. When JJ came out and saw her, he was smiling from ear to ear, and so was she. All of the feelings she had for him came back stronger than ever. Smiling and laughing, he hugged and kissed her passionately. He couldn't believe she drove all that way. They reminisced about old times and laughed. Throughout the visit, he kept saying how he was going to look out for her and Noah when he got out. He even apologized for cheating on her and said he was ready to be in a committed relationship. They were like two teenagers, so giddy and into one another, like a first date. The hours came and went quickly, and soon it was time for her to go. They hugged and kissed passionately again, and Seanette wore a huge grin all the way back home.

Since Seanette could not afford to keep driving back and forth up north to visit JJ, she told him he could call her collect more often. That was a big mistake! He started calling her every other day, with no care about her phone bill. She soon became overwhelmed because she couldn't afford his frequent calls and meet Noah's basic needs at the same time. Besides, writing him three lengthy letters—at least twenty-five to thirty pages each—three times a week should have been enough to keep him occupied, but she was wrong. JJ demanded more time. At first, it was flattering. But with the stress of school, work, taking care of Noah and everything else, she just couldn't handle JJ's neediness. She felt he should be a release for some of her tension and worries, but he was adding to them instead.

The next two years were filled with confusion and turmoil for Seanette regarding JJ. First, she found out he had been cheating on her—yes, from prison—with his old girlfriend, the same girl he cheated with the last time.

Seanette was so hurt and felt so foolish, but she couldn't make up her mind whether she should or even wanted to stay with JJ. That past Christmas, he had sent clothes for Noah and a wooden clock he had made in the prison that had their initials for the numbers. He also had a few family portraits drawn of them and, to top it all off, he got her and Noah's names tattooed on his body. That must be love, right? Wayne didn't even have his own son's name tattooed on him. In the 'hood, this was the ultimate display of affection and sacrifice.

Finally, however, Seanette just couldn't shake the feeling that JJ had made her out to be a fool. So, she put a block on her phone, stopped writing him and returned all his letters to her. Unfortunately, JJ wasn't that easy to get rid of. He just wouldn't leave her alone. When she put the block on, he just had one of his homies call her on three-way. And when she stopped writing him, his wrote even more letters to her.

Seanette was able to stand her ground for an entire year and actually forgot about JJ—that is, until Valentine's Day rolled around. She found a letter and a card in the mailbox from him and, instead of sending them back, she opened them. The truth was, it was Valentine's Day and she was lonely and curious, and she missed him. Well, JJ said the letter was his last attempt to reach her and then he would leave her alone.

Seanette felt bad. Maybe JJ really did love her. She wrote him, then he wrote back, and just like that, he was in her good graces again. She asked when he got out and he promised her he'd be home before the holidays. She thought eight or even nine more months she could do.

Well, JJ wasn't really telling the truth about his release date. During the period that they weren't talking, he had accrued more prison time for fighting. Actually, an entire year! Seanette found out through a friend who had a connection with the Correctional Department. Since JJ had been moved around to different prisons and now was much closer, when Seanette found out his real release date, she immediately went to see him. He was surprised that she knew about the fighting and explained that he didn't tell her because, he said, he didn't want her to worry and he was trying to do better. She believed him and stood by his side until his release on November 14, 2001.

Seanette was at work when JJ called her the day he got out. He was at his mother's house and she was throwing him a coming home party. Seanette was so excited. After work, she picked up Noah from daycare and stopped at home to feed and bathe him and also get herself ready. JJ called about a dozen times while she got herself together, so she just ended up talking to him until she headed out the door.

The drive to JJ's mother's house was only about fifteen minutes. Seanette parked her car and rang the security door. JJ buzzed her in, and she could hardly contain herself as she walked to the front door. Now was not the time for Noah to be lagging behind, so she picked him up and carried him on her hip the rest of the way. She only had to knock on the door once before JJ opened it.

They stayed at the party only a few minutes and then went back to her apartment. They talked the entire night and, of course, had sex. Seanette had a surprise for JJ. She had gotten his name tattooed on her body and he immediately responded by asking her to marry him. She had to decline. She had cold feet after her divorce from Wayne and all the drama that came along with it. She still could not understand how it could take only five minutes to get married, yet almost two years to get divorced. So, marriage was not something she wanted to jump into. However, while JJ said he would live with his mother, being that he paroled there, Seanette did insist he move in with her and Noah.

The "honeymoon" period of their reunion lasted for about three months, during which JJ was the perfect gentleman. He even got a job through agencies that help felons stay gainfully employed. He wasn't making a lot of money, but he was working, and Seanette was satisfied.

Then, they started arguing about money. He wanted to "hit a lick" just one last time, but Seanette was not having it and threatened to leave him if he did. He backed off on that idea.

But then Seanette found another girl's number in JJ work pants pocket, and she called her. The girl was very honest. She told Seanette that JJ had approached her and never told her he had a girlfriend. When she told Seanette that JJ had her come to his mother's house, Seanette asked if she had seen the framed pictures of herself and JJ on the walls. The girl said he had told her Seanette was his sister.

Seanette was furious. She wanted to straight bust JJ, but she didn't want a lot of drama. He usually broke and destroyed things in her house when they got into arguments. So, she decided to play it real cool. She made his favorite meal: barbecued pigs feet, greens, macaroni and cheese, and hot water cornbread. When he came home from work, she greeted him with a kiss and a smile and then fixed his plate. He was really surprised that she had cooked, and his favorite dinner at that, in the middle of the week. She poured him a glass of flavored sparkling water, massaged his shoulders and asked about his day. "I can get used to this," he remarked with a wide smile.

Seanette then nonchalantly told him a made-up story about how a girl recognized her while she was at the grocery store and said, "Tell your brother I said hi." Then, in a coy tone, Seanette added, "I asked the girl where she saw my picture, and she said at your mother's house." Immediately, JJ stood up and threw his plate of food across the room. Seanette watched as it flew, hit the wall and slid down toward the carpet. She calmly walked over to pick up the mess. That's when JJ snatched her by the waist, lifted her up, carried her to the bedroom, and threw her on the bed. "Oh, so you think it's funny? Huh?"

JJ and Seanette started wrestling on the bed as she tried to get away. Being much stronger than her, he tired her out quickly. He held her down by her wrists and told her to calm down. She closed her eyes and imagined being covered with butterflies. She envisioned herself flying high and free with her friends. She stopped struggling, but when he tried to kiss her, she turned her face away. "Oh, so you don't love me anymore?" She tried to spread her wings and soar above the clouds, but was held back by her reality. She couldn't take flight and instead just plummeted face down into the soil. She tried and tried to flutter her wings but to no avail, and she lost her will.

JJ forcibly pulled down Seanette's overalls while she still had her boots on and snatched her underwear down. She didn't know what to do. She was scared and pissed and exhausted from struggling to get away from him. However, inner strength kicked in and she found enough courage to defiantly ask him, "So, you just gonna rape me?" "You don't want to have sex with me?" JJ snickered back. "We are about to get married. You my girl, ain't you? This ain't hardly rape. This is mines. All of this is mines."

Seanette decided not to fight JJ, she just submitted to get it over with. He left her with a few bruises on her chest, arms and legs, and he bit and tore the skin off of her pocketbook in order to "leave something on her mind." JJ was very discreet about where he left bruises. He always put them where they could be covered.

He and Seanette continued to argue, fight, break up and get back together for almost six months after that. She suggested they get counseling, but he was completely against it at first. "I don't understand why we have to tell white people our problems," he would say. But Seanette insisted, telling him if he didn't go with her, they would have to go their separate ways. He then agreed but didn't show up for the first two appointments. So, Seanette started attending therapy by herself and asked him to move out.

The cycle of arguing, fighting and breaking up continued, however. And now, JJ was also stalking Seanette when they weren't together. He would show up uninvited. He broke into her apartment and subtly rearranged her things. He let air out of her tires. He left notes on her car. And he followed her. Seanette felt like she had no choice but to be with him, so she let him come back one last time.

JJ started off being overly nice, bringing home flowers, expensive purses, perfume, cell phones and other gifts for Seanette. He even tried to bribe her with money. She was not impressed. She stopped being materialistic back in high school. Well, before long, JJ was back to his old ways and started hanging out in the 'hood with his homies.

He also wanted her to sell marijuana out of her house "for some extra cash." Seanette couldn't believe he would even suggest such a thing. There was no way she was going for that. Besides the fact that she hadn't smoked marijuana in years, JJ knew the traumatic experience she had as a small child when her mother's home was raided by the police. Seanette was so angry that he had the audacity to even ask her. That was the last straw.

But how was she going to make sure he really got the message this time, for good? After the last go-round with JJ, Seanette knew he had to see that she really meant business. She was ready to physically fight him if she had to, in order to get him out of her house. Then she came up with a plan.

Early one morning, Seanette got up while JJ was still sleeping, called out of work, dropped Noah off at Janet's house, and returned to her apartment. JJ was still asleep. She reached under the mattress and pulled out the butcher knife she placed there for safekeeping.

Seanette stared at her reflection on the blade for a moment and breathed deeply. It was appalling to her that her life had come to this point, but she had to do something now. She said a small prayer, put the knife in the small of her back underneath the elastic of her sweatpants, pulled her t-shirt down and woke JJ up.

She told him firmly it was over and she wanted him to leave. This did not go over well with him. He jumped up and started arguing with her. That's when she pulled out the knife. "Oh, you goin' stab me?" he asked mockingly. He grabbed the knife out of her hand. She ran to grab her cordless phone to call the police, but he grabbed that, too. He then took the phone, ran downstairs and threw it so far that it landed in the back-yard of a neighbor all the way around the corner. While he was out of the apartment, Seanette attempted to quickly stuff his belongings in brown paper bags. By the time he came back up to the apartment, she had some his stuff outside and was about to close the door. But he pushed his way inside, now pleading with her to "just talk."

Since he seemed willing, Seanette thought maybe talking would be a better strategy at this point. She asked JJ to sit down and remain calm. She then tried to reason with him. She apologized for any wrong she had done in the relationship or to him. She told him she needed to get her life together and connect back with God and get back into therapy. He calmed down a little but was still going off about her "calling the white man on him."

JJ finally got up and left, promising to leave Seanette alone. He continued to make infrequent visits, but Seanette stood her ground. She changed the locks on her door and her phone number and made plans to move soon. Really soon. She was just so grateful that Noah was never in the house to witness these experiences.

Enjoying My Company

Ooh . . . it's a quarter 'til eight
Get ready
I don't want to be late
I'm kind of nervous
I've never done this before
Keeping my mind focused
Time to explore
No time for excuses
Running out of time
Courage and joy
I desire to find
Not certain of the destination
Tired of all the procrastination
Faith is my sight
God's love is my friend
Almost ready
No time
To start
Drifting in the past
Take one glance at the mirror
Determined to love myself
At last
In the car, the sun gently shines across my knee
While groovin to the healing
Soul-filled sound
Of India.Arie

CHAPTER 32
Self-Discovery

Despite all of her turmoil with JJ, Seanette still endeavored to redirect her attention more towards her academic goals. Her hard work paid off and she was absolutely thrilled when she found out she would be a scholarship recipient.

As a matter of fact, it was such a big boost to her self-esteem that she took a leap of faith and enrolled in a math class. She had to at least try; she couldn't keep avoiding it based solely on her past experiences in high school. It was do or die time anyway because, to get her associate's degree, she only needed ten more classes—and five of them were in math.

By the end of the semester, Seanette did very well in her speech, history and administration of justice classes, and fairly well in science. But she had a terrible experience with math. She couldn't even walk into the classroom the first two sessions, and when she finally did get the nerve, she completely spaced out. She couldn't concentrate and didn't understand the teacher at all. She started having a panic attack and left, dropping the class just in time to avoid getting a fail. She would attempt to take math two more times after that but failed both times. At this point, she was completely discouraged, so she decided to take a break from school and work more. After all, she really needed the money.

All of this turmoil with JJ and angst with school brought Seanette to an inner crossroads. She knew something was fractured in her soul, and she just wanted to be healed. She was so tired of being confused, suspicious, depressed, negative, anxious, angry and bitter. Just tired of putting herself down. Tired of hating herself. And tired of being needy. She no longer wanted low self-esteem and no longer wanted to practice self-destructive behavior. She finally reached a point in life where she wanted to embrace everything about herself. She wanted to learn how to accept her flaws as her strengths and how to enjoy her own company. She didn't just want it. She was determined to do it.

Seanette prayed and asked God to forgive her for all the times she ran ahead. She also asked for strength, courage and wisdom to forgive herself. She wrote a list of goals and dreams and asked God to do the impossible in her life, and to heal her heart and mind. She asked Him to fill her with so much of His love that she would no longer look for things or people to "fix" her. She even asked Him to make her uncomfortable with anything that was a distraction to fulfilling His purpose for her life. And she asked Him to show her how to love herself, to show her His perfect plan for her life and to not allow her to rest until it was accomplished.

Going back to church, therapy and writing were all necessary for Seanette's healing. Not just any church, but a church God wanted her in. She prayed for a church where she could grow and learn about God for real, because she wanted peace, and she wanted answers. Soon, she found a church through an old high school friend, where the young pastor seemed truly anointed and the young members were down to earth and unpretentious. She befriended a small circle of people, and they weren't fake or "churchy" but talked about real issues and their own struggles.

Being there and having fellowship with these wonderful believers gave Seanette such a sense of relief and peace. She went every Sunday and cried before, during and after pretty much every service. And each Sunday, she felt stronger and stronger.

During one service, the pastor spoke on the importance of enjoying your own company. Seanette knew this was a real problem for her. She hated to be alone or go anywhere alone. For instance, she had never been to the mall by herself, or to the movies or even to get a bite to eat.

Truth be told, she was afraid to be out alone because she was so self-conscious, she thought people were staring at her, talking about her or making fun of her.

Still, deep down inside, she really wanted to overcome this fear and learn to just enjoy her own company. Seanette wanted to go on a date by herself and, considering all that she had been through, she felt she owed it to herself. She was so emotionally drained from all her baggage and the pain was too real, but she knew in her heart she could no longer blame anyone or give someone else the burden of "fixing" her. She didn't have the energy anymore to keep trying to find herself in somebody else, and she didn't have any more to give to others—no more pointless conversation, no more fruitless encouragement, no more unappreciated sacrifice, no more one-sided love—nothing! She had gotten enough of a revelation to know that the problems were really within herself.

So, Seanette decided to go on a date with herself. And she made it a big deal!

One beautiful summer day, Seanette showered and got dressed. She decided to wear jeans, and not just any jeans. Feeling confident, she slipped on a pair of "I used to be able to get into these" jeans. She was thrilled! Her weight had severely ballooned because she had stuffed down every emotion imaginable with food. But now, no sweat pants! Wow! Now, that was a true miracle!

Seanette chose to wear her hair in its natural state. The deep waves enhanced her rich, jet-black curls as she applied water conditioner and a dab of coconut oil, to add a little shine. She reflected on how her hair always felt like a curse that made her ashamed. Some people, usually of color, always looked with disdain at her and her hair as if she had stolen it from someone, like she was unworthy or undeserving of its texture. Then came the questions, "What are you mixed with?" or, "Do you have a relaxer or perm in your hair?" Little did they know, she couldn't care less about hair, period! Countless times she would be so dejected and stressed about her hair to the point that she would take drastic measures, like getting scissors and chopping it, or shaving it off. But not today. She no longer felt shame or self-loathing. Today was different.

Before she got dressed, Seanette took a close look at herself in the mirror, a real look. Her reflection made her smile. She liked what she saw. She admired her dark complexion, rich like a chocolate bar. Brushing her face gently with the palm of her hand, she recalled how embarrassed she was as a teen because of bad acne. But despite the blemishes and scars, she was now determined to see, and appreciate, her inner beauty.

Her eyes then traveled to the tattoo on her breast. A huge, wonderful butterfly now covered what used to be JJ's name. So many thoughts about her old love flooded her mind. Quite frankly, it reminded her that the old love was still there. But she chose to focus her mind back on the present. She didn't want to dwell on the past. She was eager to experience what today might offer and refused to sabotage her uplifted mood.

While applying one of her favorite perfumed body crèmes, Seanette's attention was drawn to all the stretch marks criss-crossing her abdomen. An overwhelming sense of joy squashed the negative thoughts that tried to swirl inside her mind and spirit. She took a deep, satisfying breath as she envisioned her baby boy's smile. Despite her initial struggles with motherhood, Noah gave her so much joy without saying a word. This was unconditional love, and it was absolutely priceless. Seanette whispered a quick prayer to thank God for the gift of motherhood. Noah was her greatest blessing, and those "hideous scars" would forever be a badge of wisdom and honor to remind her that, regardless how "ugly" a situation looks, something beautiful can always come out of it.

As Seanette applied lotion to her knees, she recalled how much of a tomboy she used to be. Her knees and legs weren't smooth like the other girls. In fact, they were rough and all scarred up. Gratitude for full use of all of her limbs entered her soul. Suddenly, Seanette got a notion to paint her toes, which she had never given a thought to do before. She picked a color, a bright color called "Outrageous Orange." After all, the Southern California sun was shining bright that day.

This day, Seanette didn't care if her nail polish was outrageously bright, or her hair was full of waves and curls, or even if she was out by herself. Honestly, she was tired of hiding. She was tired of pretending. She just wanted to go outside naked and shout, "Look, everybody! This is me, the real me! Open, live and uncut!"

One thing was for sure: Seanette wanted to go on that date with herself. She had prayed for this. And now that it was finally here, she could hardly wait. Now, she was a woman who was sure of what she wanted even if she wasn't sure how to get it. She was determined to go on that date, to treat herself and to get to know herself even better. One final look in the mirror confirmed it: "I'm absolutely ravishing!"

Seanette arrived at the café around four-ish. She parked her car, walked towards the entrance and then paused just inside the door to scan the atmosphere. For a moment, she wanted to turn around and run out, but she realized too much was at stake to retreat now. Now was the time to get all the pieces back that were stolen from her all her life. Her innocence. Her dreams. Her goals. Her confidence. Her dignity. Her worth. Her purpose.

The task seemed too hard—more like impossible. Besides all the damage and abuse brought on by other people in her life, Seanette hated the decisions she had made and the times that she freely, without a care, gave away her innocence and cast her own purpose away. Gone, with no regard to the long-term impact. So, here at this restaurant by herself, she was nervous and apprehensive about it really accomplishing anything. But she also felt on top of the world! Nothing else mattered except this moment, this time. It belonged to her and her alone. She was in control, with no one to answer to but herself and God. What an opportunity!

Seanette ordered a peppermint tea. She heard it was relaxing. Literally from the first sip, she felt a release—a release from turmoil and pain, anger and confusion, doubt and low self-esteem. All that was replaced with peace, acceptance, gratitude, love and joy.

At first, she couldn't understand these new feelings overtaking her. Then it hit her. She was being introduced to herself. This was Seanette.

This was who Seanette really was. Good or bad, and whether self-induced or inflicted by others, her life experiences were things that merely happened. Period. They didn't define her. Their power over her was done. It ended that day.

Seanette took the last sip of her tea, like an unintentional, even providential symbol of the end to life the way it was. With her new-found sense of self-acceptance and joy, she closed her eyes and imagined what life was going to be like now. Radical transformation had begun.

Comfort

I am resting in a place
Where my mind is free
I am walking in grace
With a smile on my face
I am laughing
Joy overwhelms my soul
Beyond the confusion and complaining
I breathe in the stillness
Of quiet moments
I strive
To learn and grow
Led by strength and motivation
Fueled with determination for my destination
Surrounded in peace
Grounded in love

CHAPTER 33

Paying It Forward

That first date with herself was only the beginning. Seanette was enjoying her own company. After that, she treated herself to live theater, comedy shows, art museums, more dinners, malls, roller skating, bike riding, swimming and the beach all by herself. Learning to accept and appreciate herself helped her begin to live each day with expectancy and hope, no longer worrying about what was going to happen next.

During this transformation, Seanette resumed her "Dear Father God" letters. It helped her maintain and even nurture a proper, healthier perspective on God's love for her—her purpose—as she pursued her goals and passions. For instance, she also picked up writing poetry again, something she took great interest in as a young girl in school, especially after being selected for a poetry reading.

While her letters to God were more for intimate expression and connection between her and the Lord, Seanette's poetry became something that just burst out of her, almost literally. Now, she wrote all of the time, the words just pouring out of her constantly regardless of what she was doing—when she was driving, watching television, cleaning, sitting still and even in her sleep. It overwhelmed her at first, even made her a little uncomfortable because the words were coming so fast. She tried having a pen and paper always handy, but she couldn't pull them out fast enough to write all the words down as they came to her mind. So, she started writing on whatever was within reach: napkins, scrap pieces of paper and sticky notes in addition to notepads. It was like a treasure hunt adventure.

Through a mutual friend, Seanette was introduced to an editor at a local newspaper who offered her a weekly column. She also participated in local poetry slams and even did a poetry reading on public access television. But writing had become her passion. There was a fire inside of her that grew each and every time she picked up a pen. She just didn't know what to do with that passion.

She thought about pursuing writing full time, but as a single mother on a tight income, concern about Noah held her back. This could not be a viable plan for taking care of him. She really wanted to complete school in large part for his sake. He didn't ask to be here. He was innocent. She was determined to put him first and that meant a life devoted to making his life better. Getting her bachelor's degree was a big part of achieving that goal. She felt her time for writing had come and gone.

Around this time is when Seanette decided to become celibate until the right mate, her soul mate, crossed her path. She didn't want to choose the wrong person again—she wouldn't be able to handle another heartache. Besides, she was already learning to be content by herself. She was growing and learning and experiencing life with a fresh outlook. She was done looking back at life through the rear window. She was looking forward to her future. The summer had been a time of awakening for her. She had learned to be strong all by herself, and she savored every moment of it, each and every day.

Late one night, Pam called. "What time is it? Is that the phone?" Seanette wondered as she was awakened out of her sleep. "Hello?" "I miss you," her mother whispered. Pam cleared her throat. "I miss you," she repeated, more clearly. "Are you asleep?" "Uh . . . no," Seanette responded, wondering why her mother was calling her, and so late at that. "What's wrong? Is everything okay?" "Yeah, yeah, everything is fine." Seanette's mind searched for something to say. The silence was intensely uncomfortable and she didn't know how to handle it. She had never had a conversation with her mother that was empty of words.

Frankly, Seanette was apprehensive. She didn't know how the conversation might go, and she felt powerless over the entire situation. It made her feel vulnerable, and she didn't like it. The unpredictability of it all was just too much to think about. She tensed up and put up her guard. Then it came to her, maybe she should use some of the principles and techniques she learned in therapy over the past couple of years. "There is more room on the outside than the inside" and "Express your feelings with love and compassion." All the statements echoed in her mind.

But Seanette didn't have the guts to say any of them. The truth of the matter was, she was afraid to confront her mother. She didn't want to argue, so she just stayed quiet, not a word. Of course, she had the feeling that her mother was also not sure what to say or how to begin. So, Seanette just decided to let her mother express herself without any interruption, when she was ready. The silence continued.

Then, "I miss you!" Pam blurted out. This time, she was crying. Seanette struggled to maintain her composure, but still, she chose not to respond. Seanette had waited her entire life for her momma to just be honest and talk about why things were the way they were between them. Why did she act the way she did? More importantly, what was she really feeling? "This can't be it! Is this that moment I've been wanting all my life?" Seanette pondered to herself. Her heart was filled with excitement, nervousness and hope all at the same time—along side the underlying anger, hurt, bitterness and hate. "Do I hate her? Still?"

Seanette's mind raced in those silent moments on the phone. She thought about how her entire life she was taught it's okay to dislike someone's actions, but it's never okay to hate someone. So she had to check herself. But she also couldn't lie to herself. She did feel hate. But she didn't hate her mother; she hated all the things she was subjected to because of her mother's choices. That's what Seanette hated. That's what she wished she could erase away even now. She wanted to be free of it all, carried away on the fluttering wings of her childhood friend, the butterfly.

Then Seanette thought about how, in many ways, she should be proud of her mother and grateful to her for so many things. Pam had always tried to give her daughter everything that would keep Seanette grounded. She sacrificed far more than Seanette could ever comprehend, until that moment. Pam made sure she had a quality education and taught her a good work ethic, determination and strength, and even faith in God. Although her methods were hurtful and abusive at times, Pam did love her daughter. She did the best she could from what she herself had learned and been through. Seanette knew from her own experience why her mother self-medicated and practiced other self-destructive behaviors. It must have been due to all the abuse and trauma she had endured in her own life.

It was in that moment that Seanette released all unforgiveness towards her mother. She suddenly didn't care if her mother never took personal responsibility for what she had done. In that moment, by freeing her mother, Seanette freed herself.

The conversation easily picked up right after that, and momma and daughter caught up on all the missed time. They laughed and cried and reminisced.

During the time that they had not been speaking, a lot had changed in Pam's life. Besides Charles going back to prison and getting out in a year or so, Pam had offered to be caretaker for her niece Tiffany, her brother Bruce's daughter. Now, it was no secret that Bruce and Tiffany's mother Kelly were using crack cocaine together for years. Little Tiffany frequently had to spend the weekends with Pam and Seanette because of it, but she always went back home. As her parents' addiction spiraled out of control, Tiffany's wellbeing noticeably suffered. Her clothes were always tattered and dirty, her hair was unkempt, and she often got physically hurt due to lack of supervision.

After getting beat up pretty bad by a drug dealer, Bruce asked Pam to look after Tiffany until he got himself situated. He promised to get off drugs and come back for his daughter. That never happened. Kelly did try to get herself together enough for Tiffany to then go back to live with her, but it was only briefly. Kelly really struggled with her addiction, which now also included alcohol. Child Protective Services (CPS) was called and Tiffany was legally placed in Pam's care. By now, Bruce was out of the picture. Still struggling with crack cocaine, he became a wanderer and moved back to Cleveland.

Seanette and Tiffany had gotten close over the years that Tiffany would stay on the weekends. But after Seanette had moved out of

Pam's house, had Noah and gone through her drama with JJ, she had too much on her plate to dedicate any time to her little cousin. So, Tiffany was pretty much on her own under Pam's roof.

The dynamics in Pam's home started to change around the time Tiffany turned twelve years old. Pam's and Charles's relationship was basically the same, getting high and drunk, arguing and fighting, his leaving for a time and coming back, or his going to jail. And during his absences, Pam would befriend more shady characters and even allowed them to move in with her and Tiffany. These people were alcoholics and crack and meth users.

Tiffany was still under Pam's care when Pam and Seanette reconnected. Pam claimed that Tiffany was rebelling, so she thought it would be a good idea to send her to Cleveland for a while, "to teach her a lesson." Seanette expressed her disagreement. She knew this was a horrible idea. She asked her mother exactly what Tiffany did that was so horrible. Pam never offered an explanation, just that Tiffany lied a lot. Sure, Tiffany did have an issue with lying, but Seanette didn't understand how that constituted a reason for shipping her off. Nevertheless, Pam's mind was made up. She even lied herself and said Bruce was off drugs and Tiffany was going to live with him while there. As soon as the school year was over, she sent Tiffany to Cleveland. She was there for an entire school year.

Tiffany went through many transitions during her time in Cleveland. She stayed with Bruce for a while but had to leave when he and his girlfriend fell out. He then had her staying place to place, making her living situation incredibly unstable. When all other options finally ran out, he took her to her grandmother Myrtle's house.

Though Myrtle was now much older, she was still Myrtle. She subjected Tiffany to a lot of verbal and emotional abuse, having no problem calling her vulgar names. Tiffany's cousins were equally cruel to her and bullied her, just like Seanette's cousins did to her when Pam shipped her back there as a child. Tiffany's grades were suffering, as was her overall wellbeing. She was not doing well at all and, as could be expected, she was starting to engage in risky behaviors.

Seanette asked Pam if Tiffany could return to California and even volunteered to raise her. Pam refused. "You can pick her up from the airport, and she can stay with you for the weekend, but she needs to come back to this house by Sunday."

Interestingly, during Tiffany's time in Cleveland, Pam continued to receive monthly checks from CPS. Since her case was under guardianship, a social worker no longer conducted home visits, so they had no idea Tiffany was gone, and Pam wasn't about to report it and lose that income.

Seanette had a bad feeling about her little cousin returning to Pam's house, and she had an even worse feeling about her staying in Cleveland. In fact, she had a bad dream about Tiffany a couple of nights before Pam told her about it. Seanette was well aware of what was going on and knew what she had to do. She knew that just standing on the sidelines not offering any additional support to Tiffany was not an option. She just didn't want to tell her mother yet what she was going to do. She told Pam she wanted Myrtle's phone number so that she could talk to Tiffany and gauge her. She planned to call as soon as she hung up with Pam.

Knowing the conversation could go south really quickly, Seanette braced herself and tried to remain calm as the phone at Myrtle's rang several times. She decided to take the humble, overly amiable approach. Someone finally picked up the phone. "Who 'dis?" She recognized the voice. It was her cousin Jonah. "Hey, it's 'Nette. Is Tiffany there?" "Who is that on the phone?" she heard Myrtle yelling in the background. "It's 'Nette. She's asking for Tiffany." "I don't know why she calling here," Myrtle quipped. "That girl ain't nothing but a liar. She ain't but trouble." Myrtle proceeded to yell out obscenities as Jonah passed the phone to Tiffany.

"Hello?" Tiffany said in a dismal voice. "Hey, Tiff, this is 'Nette. I just want you to answer the questions 'yes' or 'no,' okay?" "Okay," Tiffany said as she started to cry. "I spoke to your aunt and she said you want to come back to California. Is this true?" "Yes," Tiffany responded. "Okay, do you want to live back with your aunt?" "No." Seanette then asked her, "Do you want to live with me and Noah?"

"Yes." Tiffany replied. Seanette wanted her cousin to understand what that would mean. "Tiffany, you know my life has changed. I am not for any foolishness. I need to know you are ready and will follow my rules." Tiffany responded, "I will." "Okay. I will be there to pick you up from the airport. I didn't tell your aunt that you would be coming to live with me, so don't tell anyone." "Okay, I won't."

Seanette immediately called Pam back and told her she had spoken to Tiffany and would pick her up from the airport.

Seanette picked Tiffany up on a Saturday morning and drove her straight to her house. Tiffany was very distraught and cried the entire forty-minute drive. She didn't talk much, and this concerned Seanette. She gave her Noah's room and gave her some space to settle in.

Later that evening, Tiffany shared with Seanette that she experienced some physical abuse by Pam while she was in her home. She also disclosed that one of the boyfriends Pam had while Charles was in jail tried to molest her and exposed himself naked to her. She also confirmed that Pam was still using drugs. That was all the reassurance Seanette needed to know that her plan to keep Tiffany was the right thing to do.

The next day, Seanette got a call from her mother, wanting to know when she was bringing Tiffany to her house. Seanette told her she was not bringing Tiffany there and that Tiffany did not want to live with her. Pam was furious. She demanded Seanette bring Tiffany there immediately. But for the sake of her little cousin, Seanette stood her ground. Her mother then cursed her out and hung up the phone.

But Pam wasn't giving up that easily. She ended up bringing Tiffany's mother Kelly to Seanette's house. She went through the trouble to find Kelly to use her as a ploy. Seanette refused to open the door in spite of the rukus Pam and Kelly were making. Instead, she turned on some gospel music in an effort to calm both Tiffany and Noah. "If you don't open this door, I am going to call Wayne and tell him you are an unfit mother," Pam threatened. "He's going to take Noah away from you, and you will never see him again, I will see to it! I'm going to get the police. You will never get away with this!" Then Kelly said, in a mousy voice, "Tiffany, open up the door, it's your mom."

Both Seanette and Tiffany were in disbelief by the entire scene. They couldn't understand why Pam was so angry and threatening to take Noah away, because even she had to know it was in Tiffany's best interest for her to stay with Seanette. And Kelly? Why did Pam involve her? She knew all that had happened to Tiffany while she was in Kelly's care. It was all just so bizarre.

Seanette tried to remain calm as Tiffany and Noah were now scared and crying. Pam and Kelly had left, but then Pam returned, like she promised, with the police. When the officers interviewed Tiffany, she told them that Pam physical and emotional abused her. Seanette supported her claims and also told them about Pam's crack cocaine and alcohol addictions. Seanette went on to say that Pam was an impulsive person who used severe corporal punishment as a disciplinary method, with Tiffany describing to them how Pam hit her with pots, pans, belts and extension cords.

While the police interviewed Tiffany, Pam remained on the other side of the door, demanding for Tiffany to be released into her custody. "I have guardianship papers from CPS on her," she insisted. "I want you to call the lieutenant. Clearly, you don't know how to do your job." Not long after, the lieutenant showed up with about eight officers and interviewed Tiffany. She did not recant. She stood by her story. Clearly convinced, the lieutenant then informed Seanette that Tiffany would have to go with the police and be placed in protective custody and that CPS would contact Seanette as to her cousin's whereabouts.

Seanette, Tiffany and Noah began to weep. Before Tiffany left with the police, Noah asked to pray for her. As the lieutenant and the eight officers all stood in a circle behind them, Noah asked God to return her home safely.

It was about one o'clock in the morning when Seanette received the call from the social worker. He arrived with Tiffany within half an hour. He reviewed all the required documents to hand over care to Seanette and had her sign them. Seanette was now a single mother of two.

Taking care of two children on an already overextended, fixed income proved to be almost impossible for Seanette, especially for the first ninety days. She tried to call her mother for help, as Pam was still receiving CPS checks, but Pam refused. "Since you decided to take her, you take care of her." Thankfully, Noah's father Wayne started paying child support.

Seanette initially enrolled Noah in a private Christian school and had planned to enroll Tiffany, too, but needed help paying for it. Again, she called Pam. This time, her mother agreed to help, but only offered to give her half of the CPS checks. Frustrated and at a loss for words, Seanette had no choice but to enroll Tiffany into a public school. It hurt Seanette because she remembered how much she benefitted from going to private school and she wanted Tiffany to grow up with that same benefit.

Meanwhile, Seanette was able to look for a bigger apartment, as where they were living was too small for the three of them, and the area had really begun to go downhill. She had to pull Noah out of private school in order to afford a higher rent, but it was so worth the sacrifice. Seanette and the kids moved into a three-bedroom townhome-style apartment in the Northridge area of the San Fernando Valley, without her having to work excessive overtime. Things were looking up.

Seanette was gearing up to return to school and finally knock out those last ten classes. She was so ready to transfer to a four-year university. But it meant that she had to stop writing and all activities that were not directly related to work or school. This saddened her, but she knew it was necessary in order to focus on the children.

Tiffany was soon doing better and had started therapy and seemed to be adjusting well. The transition to a new school was hard on Noah because of the friendships he had formed for two years at his previous school. Seanette hated having to make such hard decisions, but the little savings she had were used on giving Tiffany a descent wardrobe and self-care items before school started. Seanette's finances were a constant stressor for her, especially since she did not begin receiving her CPS stipend for three months.

Despite all the stress, Seanette tried to remain level-headed through it all for the sake of Noah and Tiffany. She made sure they spent a lot of family time together and they all played made-up games, did arts and crafts, went to the library to rent movies, and did other fun activities. The three of them became inseparable. Plus, they went to church every Sunday, which sustained their faith in God and helped Seanette keep her sanity. Indeed, church was a solid foundation for her, as there would be many changes in the next two years that would shake her faith to the core.

You are God

I reminisce about the times
I caught a glimpse of Him
Dancing in the wind
He rides on a cloud
He speaks peace to my mental chaos
I have birthed serenity
He sweeps me off my feet
By romancing me
With the aroma of wild honeysuckle
After a rain storm
I feel like a fairytale princess
He is such an authentic Artist
While I'm in the valley
He paints a promise
Designed into a rainbow
Formed just for me
I am basking in His love
He woos me
After a long day of work
By strategically placing a full moon
In the sky so deep
With stars sporadically placed so wide
Into the universe
So vast, far beyond
The natural eye
My heart flutters with surprise
He takes my breath away
I'm in love
He knows my name

I'm in love
My apparent fears
My frantic worries
I'm so overwhelmed
With His love
For this second
This moment
In time
I am convinced
I have fallen
I am in love

CHAPTER 34
Embracing the Journey

As Seanette continued to struggle with maintaining a household, Wayne abruptly stopped paying child support for Noah. She picked up a second job, but still never had enough money. She started a candy house selling incense, candy and other goodies to kids in the neighborhood. She still didn't have enough money. She got an additional job working third shift. She still didn't have enough money for rent, utilities, food, the kids' needs or even gas.

Through it all, though, she kept her faith strong in God. Somehow, some way, all of their needs were met. Either an unexpected check came in the mail, someone donated food or money out of the blue or some other miracle happened. In fact, this began to happen so regularly that when the mail came, they all just expected a miracle. Seanette even started finding dimes out of the blue. At first, she didn't think anything of it, but then they started turning up everywhere. Soon, even the kids were finding them. It didn't matter where they'd find them — in the grocery store, at the library, walking down the street, at the laundromat. Dimes were everywhere. Seanette started collecting them and it was always enough money for some light groceries, laundry, gas or lunch for the kids.

These miracles helped grow Seanette's, Tiffany's and Noah's faith and bonded them together. They learned how to be content and make the best out of any situation, and they were happy because they had each other. Whenever Seanette became too overwhelmed, she retreated to her room by herself to pray and cry out to God for help.

Now with three jobs, Seanette only had Sundays off. Between her 40-plus hours a week job at the group home and then working at the kids' afterschool program until the evenings Monday through Friday, and then working at the post office from nighttime to early the next morning from Thursday to Saturday, her grueling work schedule had her stressed out to the max. On those last days of the week, she even had to sleep and change clothes in the car. Thankfully, Tiffany was old enough to watch Noah and so Seanette relied on her to feed him, bathe him and make sure he went to bed on time. Also, Seanette was able to make sure they completed their homework while at the afterschool program.

Still, she knew she just couldn't go on like this for long. She was always tired and still always late on her bills, and they were regulars at the local food and church pantries.

Seanette prayed constantly for guidance and strength. She searched for the answer within herself, even applying for jobs out of state and packing up her apartment as a stance of faith. But either she wouldn't hear back or was told she didn't qualify. She applied for food stamps, but she was turned down because she owned a car. She was going to apply for low-income housing but was told the wait list was so long, she wouldn't hear anything for several years. Then she applied for subsidized housing but was turned down because she made too much money and was turned down a second time after she appealed. This frustrated her to no end. She knew she had to return to school but didn't know exactly how to do it and still take care of the kids.

Still, although her situation looked bleak, Seanette never lost her faith. She knew somehow, some way, God would provide. In the meantime, she figured she would just keep working the three jobs until God made it clear what course of action she should take.

Her new-found determination caused Seanette to lose a lot of friends. They just didn't understand, her isolation from them was nothing personal; she just grew in a different direction. With two other innocent people depending on her, people who didn't ask to be here, she had to keep it together to provide them with a stable home environment. She knew they were watching how she responded to the circumstances they faced together. Since she took on all responsibility for them, she had to keep them safe and well. Knowing what it was like growing up in a chaotic household, she was not willing to expose them to unhealthy behavior.

Seanette believed she would be married one day. But she felt it would selfish, irresponsible and foolish to be dating at this point. So she stayed single, continuing to keep her promise to remain celibate and committing her life to her family and God. At first, it didn't bother her too much because she didn't have time to be distracted with thoughts of companionship. She was just trying to keep her head above water while maintaining her sanity. To alleviate her loneliness, confusion and anger, she started writing her "Dear Father God" letters again, something that had taken a back seat during her financial woes and overwhelming work schedule. She even started journaling again, which became very therapeutic and helped her resolve to remain celibate until the right man came along, no matter how long it took.

Then one day, her mother's friend Lucy called. When Seanette heard Lucy's voice on the other line, she assumed something must have happened to her mother. Not exactly. "Girl, yo' momma 'bout to get paid," Lucy said. "Charles got out of prison, and he is not doing well. He 'bout to die! Yo' momma needs you now more than ever."

Seanette was sick to her stomach. "What did she just say?" she thought to herself. After the whole skirmish around Tiffany, it had been four years since Seanette and her mother had spoken.

Seanette asked to talk to her mother. "Hello?" Pam whimpered. "What happened to Charles? Where is he now?" Seanette asked. "He's upstairs sleeping," her mother replied. She explained to Seanette that Charles was very sick with cancer and had also lost his eyesight. His organs were all shutting down and he had to go to the hospital every few days to get fluid drained out of his liver. He couldn't even use the bathroom by himself. She also said that Charles had just gotten out of jail a couple of days prior and that, when she picked him up from the bus stop, he was walking very slowly and his stomach was swollen. Then she added, "The doctor had given him less than six weeks to live.

We have to take a taxi everywhere, because we don't have a car. Can you come over?"

Seanette was in shock. The man who had caused so much pain, dysfunction and turmoil in their home was now helpless and . . . dying? It was surreal. She knew everyone had to die, but wow! Cancer! Seanette took a month's leave from her job at the group home to help her mother with Charles during the day. She took them regularly to the doctor, grocery shopping and the pharmacy. She did whatever her mother asked of her.

Charles's health continued to decline at a rapid rate and before long, he was receiving hospice care. Seanette made all his funeral arrangements, including agreeing to get a loan to pay it. Pam asked her to, as the life insurance policy wouldn't cash out until six to eight weeks after his death. Seanette had just recently paid her car off, so she got a small loan of five thousand dollars in exchange for the title.

But Seanette was strategic about this. When she took her mother to the mortuary to make all the final arrangements, Seanette first had a private meeting with just herself and the program manager to explain how she had to use her car to secure the loan to pay for everything. So, during the meeting with Pam, the program manager had Pam sign a waiver that secured a portion of the life insurance proceeds for Seanette. Of course, Pam had no idea what she was signing. She was too high.

Pam continued to stay high all through Charles' time in hospice care, even drinking his morphine medication. She also had a lot of hangers-on and dope dealers around frequently. They were all high every time Seanette went over her mother's house to help with Charles. This made it very difficult for her to be around her mother, let alone handle Charles' affairs. Pam put all the responsibilities on her, taking advantage of the fact that, as usual, Seanette felt an overwhelming sense of guilt and obligation to help her.

However, Seanette grew increasingly frustrated by it. Her mother's dismissive, manipulative behavior became a huge trigger for her that finally resulted in an explosive argument. Seanette told her mother she hated her. She told her she hated everything Pam ever put her through.

She told her she hated that Pam was on drugs. She told her she hated that Pam hung around lowlife people. She told her she hated that Pam refused to take responsibility for any of her actions, past and present.

Shortly after Charles died, Pam moved to Cleveland to live with her mother Myrtle and the rest of her siblings. A few weeks went by without a word between her and Seanette. But once she received the payout from Charles' life insurance company and saw that they had already paid Seanette five thousand dollars in effect reimbursing her for the cost of the loan she secured for the title to her car—Pam was furious and called her. She became even more irate to learn that Seanette had already used the money to pay the loan back, plus interest, and got the title to her car back. Pam cursed Seanette out for taking her money. Three years would pass before they spoke again.

In spite of the insurance company's five thousand dollar payout to Seanette, her financial woes grew worse. No matter how many hours she worked, she never had enough money. To help with the bills, Tiffany enrolled in a public charter high school and got a part-time job. But they still didn't have enough money. This reality left Seanette with no choice but to move out of the three-bedroom townhouse into a one-bedroom apartment and give away her bedroom set and other things to condense all of their belongings. She purchased two twin-size mattresses and put them on the floor in the bedroom, one for her and Noah and the other for Tiffany. They made the best of what they had, the best of their circumstances, all the way through to the time of Tiffany's graduation from high school and then going out on her own.

After Tiffany graduated and moved out, Seanette decided the time was right to return to school. She knew she was getting nowhere with working excessive hours at dead-end jobs, sacrificing so much for so little in return. She knew she needed to make a drastic, life-altering change. The signs were written pretty clearly on the wall and time was of the essence to finally get started on her dreams and be tenacious in order for it all to work. Getting a college degree was the first step.

So, Seanette quit her job at the group home and the swing shift job at the post office in order to attend school full time. She cashed out her 401(k) to help with finances and enrolled Noah into a free healthcare plan, since she lost her coverage when she resigned. She was confident this was the best path for things to get better for her and Noah, especially now that Tiffany was grown and living on her own. It had been eight years since Seanette dropped out of school while in the midst of her ups and downs with her last "flame," JJ. Now, eight years later, she was ready to put all of that behind her. She was determined to not only go back to school but, this time, she would finish.

A friend suggested that Seanette be tested for a learning disability to address her issues with math. "A learning disability?" She pondered the thought. If she did have one, that would explain a lot! She met with an admissions counselor at the local community college and inquired about the Disabled Student Services program. The counselor had her contact the professor in charge and one of the things he explained was that the testing was conducted in two-part intervals because the entire test would take a total of six hours.

Fear tried to creep up in Seanette's heart, but she allowed perseverance to clothe her mind and spirit. She was determined to face math head on. She was ready to conquer her fear and recover her future. It was grueling, but she endured the test and the results concluded that she did in fact have a learning disability. While her scores soared in English and reading-related subjects, it was determined that she had an equivalent of a 5th grade education in math. She was actually quite relieved because it all made sense now.

Being part of Disabled Student Services helped Seanette tremendously. The college provided tutoring, she was allowed to take all timed tests in the library, she had priority registration and more scholarships were available to her. Things were really changing for the better for Seanette. She was even able to quit her part-time job at the after-school program because she ended up getting work on campus.

Eventually, Seanette successfully completed all of her math requirements. Yes, she struggled and failed a couple of math courses two additional times, but she finally passed all five required math courses. The year was 2008 and she was now poised to receive her associate's degree! Plus, during the same semester, she landed a job with a local government Child Protective Services agency.

And if things weren't already good enough, a couple of days before graduating, Seanette was informed by the scholarship foundation that she had a credit balance remaining on her scholarship. It was enough to cover her first two semesters at a four-year university! Also, she was going to be able to receive another scholarship after she transferred. All in all, Seanette was able to plan it so that, with those scholarship funds, combined with financial aid, Pell grants and private donors, she was going to be able to earn her bachelor's degree without going into any debt. She wouldn't have to pay a dime!

As Seanette prepared to start at the university in the fall, Noah was now eleven and would soon enter middle school. He was also doing well and his grades were good. He was also playing all kinds of sports, including golf, swimming, football, basketball, track and soccer, and thanks to a wonderful support system of fellow church members, friends and colleagues, Seanette had plenty of help transporting him to and from his practices and games while she handled her school work. Finally, everything had come together nicely.

The first day of school at the university finally arrived. The crisp fall breeze sent a chill down Seanette's spine. As she locked her car door and crossed the street, she gathered her scarf around her neck and tugged at the zipper of her pullover sweater. She couldn't afford a parking permit, so she had to park on a surface street on the other side of campus. Oh, well. This gave her lots of time to think. God knows she did that way too much! She began the long trek.

Seanette didn't have a "real" winter coat. Not yet, anyway. "That will be one of the first things I'll buy when I get my check," she mused to herself, suddenly realizing that was just one more thing to add to her list after the rent, the light bill, the gas bill, groceries, and a new jacket for Noah. "Oh, and he needs some more pants." She felt the stress and anxiety begin to grip her heart. But then she refused to lose this special moment for herself. Instead, she let excitement envelope her as she continued towards her first class at a four-year university.

Tears began welling up in her eyes. She could not believe she made it here at last! Man, it had been a long road. She thought about all the times she felt this dream had been defeated, like when she had to postpone it in order to provide for both Noah and Tiffany, and prior to that, when she kept self-sabotaging with her destructive behavior.

But then, negative mental chatter about her new job began to flood her mind. "You're just a clerk. It's only by the grace of God you even got that job. You don't have a 'real' degree, just an associate's degree from a community college." She looked around the campus for a moment and immediately felt so out of place. Everyone seemed to have their lives together, all educated and professional. But that just made her think about how people assumed she was some kind of administrator because she dressed professionally at work. She learned that from Diane. They just didn't know most of her clothes came from Goodwill.

Then Seanette thought about how she usually sat alone in the break room at work and read items on the bulletin board to pass the time. She then recalled how one day her eyes were drawn to a particular flier that indicated her employer would pay for a master's degree, and how, right away, fear and self-doubt tried to take hold. "Should I apply? I'm not smart enough. They probably won't even pick me. I haven't been here long, and there is probably a long list." She had then determined to work past that fear, too.

Seanette continued to walk across the campus. Wow! This was a long walk!

What a tragedy it was when James, the longtime boyfriend of Seanette's "play "Aunt Janet, passed away. She didn't go to the funeral because she was afraid of seeing JJ, but she did send flowers. Frankly, after all of his possessiveness and stalking, Seanette didn't want to be harassed. It also didn't help that she ran into him a few weeks prior. He insisted on taking her to dinner, and she went. He offered to pay, but she only had water. He told her he had been shot several times and was on medication because he had lost some of the mobility in his hands. All the rest of the time, he told her how he was ready for a committed relationship. He kept going on about how now was the time to get married and settle down. Of course, he needed to divorce his wife first.

At the end of dinner, JJ gave Seanette his phone number and asked her to call. After that night, she didn't know what to think. She stored his number in her cell phone, but only because she couldn't bring herself to throw it away. "Maybe he did change," she wondered. "Should I wait for him? He said he got a job, and now, since he has kids, his life had changed. He wasn't surprised that I graduated, either." In fact, he told Seanette that was exactly why they needed to be together, because she wanted something out of life — unlike his wife who, he said, didn't do anything but smoke marijuana all day.

After all, Seanette continued to think, JJ was upset that she had covered up her tattoo of his name, while he still had his with her and Noah's names, saying he would never cover them up. "I love you for life. You are my queen. You know that." She thought, "Maybe if he sees what I'm doing with my life, then he will try to change his for the better." But then she thought, "I don't want to blow my years of celibacy on him. He knows already that I haven't been with anyone since him. Too bad I can't say the same about him."

Then she came to her senses, "I've got to focus. I can't think about JJ now."

Seanette glanced down at her cell phone to check the time. "Great, now I'm late. Man, how much further is it? I hope I'm not lost." Oh, man! Her thoughts were everywhere. "I should have written in my journal today. Well, at least I worked out. I can't believe I've lost over seventy pounds. God, please help me keep it off." She thought about how she worked out three times a week for sixteen months.

And then Seanette thought about the new guy she met at work. Well, they had not actually met, per se. They had never been formally introduced. He just sat a few cubicles away from her, and they always smiled at each other when they passed in the hallway. He always dressed nice and neat and his clothes were always starched, he must take them to the cleaners. "And he smells good, too," Seanette added in her mind. "I don't know what cologne he wears, but I like it."

He was such a nice and polite man. Seanette noticed how he sure did sound professional on the phone with his clients. Plus, he gave everyone a holiday card for Valentine's Day, Easter and Christmas. And he always gave out the really expensive chocolates, too. Seanette never heard of Godiva until he gave her one in a card. "He is out of my league. He's probably already married, or has a girlfriend, or is at least dating someone. Who am I fooling? I have way too much baggage." She had a job, not a career, and was a divorced single parent still living in the same one-bedroom apartment for the past five years. Plus, she was a woman almost in her mid-thirties, who had been through hell and back, and who still had disappointments and unanswered questions about her life.

"I'm doing it again." Seanette constantly battled with herself to stay positive. Still, with practice, she was already getting better about not dwelling on the "what if's" in life.

Then, she suddenly thought about the butterflies, her tried and true friends that offered her an escape at her most tragic, painful and difficult times in her life. Honestly, she hadn't thought about them for quite a while. They were still her friends, but just weren't needed anymore. Seanette had nothing else to escape from now but her own self-doubts.

She stopped and looked up at the numbers on the side of the building. Then, she took a deep breath and gazed for a moment at the sky. It was a clear evening, and the stars shone brightly. "Well, this is it." She opened the glass door, went to the first classroom on the right, and walked in confidently.

Acknowledgments

To my husband Anthony, you are my soul mate, lover and best friend. You have made me a better person! I love you so much. Thank you for supporting every dream in my heart. Thank you for wiping away every tear from my eyes. Thank you for praying for me when I didn't understand or when I didn't have the strength to pray for myself. Thank you for pushing me when I felt I couldn't go on. I cannot imagine my life without you. You've got the best of my love! I love you always, Halo.

To my mother, thank you for allowing God to use you as a vessel in my life. I have learned so many lessons about God's grace and love though everything we have experienced, together and apart. You were the first person who instilled in my heart the bare essential of life: JESUS. For that I am truly forever grateful. I love you always.

To my father, who taught me through our experiences the power of forgiveness. I love you always.

To my Aunt Marguerite, I can't even begin to tell you how much you mean to me. You have held my secrets in your heart for many, many years. Thank you for loving and understanding me even through my pain. Thank you for teaching me how to laugh through my tears and sorrow. I am so grateful to God for sending you as my aunt, my prayer partner and my confidant. I love you!

To my spiritual sister Tonya, thank you for your unconditional love and support. You believed in my dreams when I had no one. I have not forgotten one hundred-fold! I love you!

To my twin in the spirit Marquita, I love you! Thank you for always being there, keeping my secrets, being willing to fast, pray, laugh and cry with me, but most of all, for being real!

To my best friend and matron of honor Jameelah, I know God ordained and placed you into my life! J, meeting you was one of the best things that ever happened to me! We were both waiting for God to send our husbands, and we were both honest about our struggles as single parents of young boys. You have always put me in my place when I was wrong and supported me through every major decision and experience. I love you, friend!

To my ride-or-die chick Kaharra, you taught me self-love and the importance of being yourself. You also were waiting on the Lord to send your husband. You are such a beautiful person inside and out! You freely give genuine love, support and respect to each and every person. You are a prayer warrior and a great woman of faith. I am so grateful to have you in my life! I love you!

To my sounding board and help-me-get-my-life-sister Nicole W., thank you for the laughs and tears. Thank you for reminding me who I am when I felt afraid or unsure. Thank you for spearheading my glam squad and teaching me how to embrace all of my curves and how to have fun while learning how to love my beautiful, unique body designed by God. I love you!

To my spiritual parents and mentors Papa Jack and "Momma" Alva, thank you for accepting me as your own child. Thank you for all of your support to my family. Thank you for the prayers and pep talks. Thank you for loving me through all seasons of my life. Thank you for walking beside me when I dared to put to action my "radical and crazy" faith. Thank you for teaching me I am worthy and deserve a wonderful life! I love you both!

To my publisher "Momma" Willa, it has been quite a ride! Thank you for not giving up on me when I was afraid or when I said quite frequently, "I don't want to finish this book." Your patience, prayers and gentle reminders helped me through some of the darkest days of my life! Thank you for helping breathe life into one of many of my dreams so that it has become a physical manifestation! Thank you for teaching me how to embrace all the blessings God has for my life. I am so grateful for you! I love you!

To my "Momma" Sydney, thank you for teaching me that I can have whatever I desire in life. Thank you for teaching me the importance of dressing my best, even on my worst day, and for helping me open my heart to receive love. Thank you for all your support and love. I love you!

To my "Momma" Michelle, thank you for teaching me how to go with the flow. Thank you for teaching me, "To thine own self be true." Thank you for reminding me that I am fully equipped with the tools, love and determination inside of me to accomplish every dream in my heart. Thank you for your unwavering support and love! I love you!

To my book reviewers:

Heather K. Jones, I am forever grateful to God for sending you into my life. You taught me that I had a choice! What a concept! I never knew I had the right to choose. Thank you for being so transparent and loving. Thank you for believing in me and reviewing my book. I am so, so honored to have met you. Thank you for sharing your wisdom and love with the world. I love you!

Professor Vickie Jensen, I am honored to know you! Your brilliance and dedication to service are amazing! You taught me I could obtain any dream. It was your guidance that fueled my faith to continue my education. You unleashed the passion of learning in my soul! Thank you for believing in me! Thank you for reviewing my book. I love you!

To every child or person I have had the pleasure of meeting or establishing a relationship with, remember, it's never as bad as it seems. Follow your dreams, and always remember, YOU ARE NEVER ALONE! God always has your back!

Have I not commanded you? Be strong and courageous. Do not be afraid; do not be discouraged, for the Lord your God will be with you wherever you go.

(Joshua 1:9 NIV)

Follow Nicole

Nicole's motto is to daily inspire, to empower, to motivate and to encourage others to make peace with their health and wellness journey through her transparency, humor, support and positivity.

You can follow Nicole on the following social media platforms:

Instagram: @tazznicc9614

Facebook: MsNyckki Cervantes

Twitter: Nyckki Cervantes, MSW

Website: www.MsNyckkiC.com